FROM INTENT TO IMPACT

The 5 Dualities of Diversity and Inclusion

MONICA DIAZ

FROM INTENT TO IMPACT

The 5 Dualities of Diversity and Inclusion by Mónica Díaz

Print: 978-1-944027-70-4

Published in the United States by Networlding Publishing

www.networlding.com

TABLE OF CONTENTS

AUTHOR'S NOTE

This book is a business memoir about what I've learned in the practice of diversity and inclusion (D&I). As with all memoirs, the events mentioned in this book are as I remember them. They are not recorded events. They are personal moments, insights, and lessons that impacted me profoundly throughout my career. They are the kinds of stories, events, and tips I would share when coaching a leader or mentoring a new colleague.

While I have taken some literary license with the dialogue, I believe the conversations depicted accurately capture the essence of the moment and the learning derived from them. I have changed the names of the people who were part of the stories, to maintain their privacy. In most cases, I have also omitted the names of the companies where each experience took place, because such events could have happened in other organizations as well.

Memoirs aren't specifically about how to do something, but I have included some practical tools in some of the chapters and in the appendix. I am confident that the stories, research, and lessons I share in this book will help you reach your highest level of impact in leading across human differences, in the most inclusive way possible.

PREFACE

Even if you don't realize it, you're on the front lines of one of the most demanding, complex, frightening, and potentially world-changing challenges of this new century.

In a world where social interactions and individual perspectives can be known around the world in an instant, it has become imperative for people to be conscious not only of how others see them, but also of how they see themselves. It is critical to know what you stand for, and how quickly you can learn about yourself and others. These skills will determine how you choose to lead your life, your family, your team, and your business.

The real challenge of understanding human differences, of diversity and inclusion, isn't out there in the world. It's not in society. It's in *you*. And the changes that are necessary are taking place inside of you, and me. Pay attention. Before you can understand and appreciate the value of human differences for what they are, what they *really* mean to you, it's necessary to have a deeper understanding of your *own* diversity—and the ways in which you're different from others.

I'm referring to an immersive understanding of yourself, one that includes the space you occupy in a world that exists outside your own life experience. Before you can create work environments where every person truly has an opportunity to thrive, where differences spark creativity and innovation, not only conflict, you must turn inward.

Our life and work experiences may be different, but if you're reading this book, they have converged. From this moment on, we can walk side by side on the rediscovery of yourself and of others around you. No matter why you think you picked up this book, your inner leader knew you needed it.

MAYBE YOU?

Your decision to start reading this book may come from a general curiosity about the title. Or maybe you're a Human Resources or diversity and inclusion (D&I) strategist who has worked on this field for some time, who has applied many best practices, and wants to know where to go next.

You may also be what we in HR call a "diverse talent." In the US, this term typically refers to women and racial/ethnic minorities, who have been historically underrepresented in higher ranks of leadership. You're the talent companies keep looking for, with good intentions and dedicated strategies, but not always tangible results and impact. As an employee and even as a leader, you may have perceived intolerance, bias, or outright hostility toward your race, your ethnicity, or the language you speak when your emotions run high. Maybe your sexual orientation has been mocked, questioned, or judged. Or perhaps the disabilities you live with every day, the faith you profess, or any other characteristic that defines who you are have made you look or feel very different from the majority of people you work with.

Maybe you're a business leader responsible for a global workforce, who needs to reach a more diverse segment of your customer base. Maybe you're among those who keep hearing the D&I conversation from the sidelines, or seeing it in the headlines. At this point, it may have become "noise" to you, because you might be convinced that you don't have a role in it, can't contribute, or can't change it in your favor. Maybe you're somehow concerned about the topic, but have learned to be extremely cautious about saying or doing anything that might get you in trouble, or put you on someone's radar. Or maybe you're just trying to figure out how to understand people who are different from you, in one or many ways, without "ruffling any feathers."

If any of these descriptions apply to you, you may also be seeking knowledge that can help you unlock the power, positive impact, and business performance that research has attributed to D&I. And here you are—exactly where you need to be. You're the one I wanted to talk to. You're the reason I wrote this book. So, I want to be sure you know what to expect from it.

As you read about intent and impact, about the five dualities of diversity and inclusion, you'll most likely have a wide variety of reactions. I recommend that you get ready to do the following:

- Acknowledge your immediate reactions and reflect on the stories and insights I've gathered for you.

- Know that you will agree with some points and disagree with others. In many instances, you will feel inspired, encouraged, and enthusiastic. In others, you may be challenged, triggered, or angered. That's normal, and I'm counting on your reactions, because positive or negative, they are the beginning of awareness, change, and growth.

- When you read the questions I pose to you, understand that many of the answers are within you. But keep in mind you may need to look for those answers in areas of your mind that bring emotions and responses you may have not wanted to reveal before, or that you're not comfortable examining. Look anyway.

That is the reality of addressing our differences. Acknowledge your thoughts, your emotions, and the actions you consider taking as you read the book. Don't run away from them. Don't ignore them. Don't dismiss them. I encourage you to keep reading. The space between a strong reaction and the moment after it is where the greatest learnings reside.

I would be remiss if I did not make it clear that this book is not just for leaders of a certain gender, race, or ethnicity in the D&I space. It's for *all* leaders, including the vast majority of leaders who are white men. Leaders who *get* the most respect are the ones who *give* the most respect. So, if you're a white man, don't think "this book is not for me." Many of the insights I will share with you came from working with stellar white men. They were senior leaders who excelled in their ability to learn about and leverage differences to create inclusive work environments that sparked innovation. They didn't "get it right" all the time, but they were leaders who "get it" when it comes to D&I.

WHO ARE THE LEADERS
WHO "GET IT"?

"How did you get it?" This is a common question used in the D&I field. When we say that a leader really gets it, it means they have developed the awareness, insight, or sensitivity to understand the continuum of the dualities I will identify and describe in this book.

When I ask leaders, "How did you get it?" I never know what I'm going to hear. I don't know because there is no typical, average, normal, or prescribed experience that ensures a great awakening in anyone. Things, events, and people of seemingly no consequence can impact a life forever. These leaders would inevitably and unequivocally tell me, "Well, I had an experience of this, this, and that," or "It was something I lived through when I was growing up," or "I made a trip that impacted me profoundly."

Chris was one of those leaders who gets it. Diversity and inclusion had intersected his life at an early age, changing him forever. Chris is a tall white man, who is now a C-suite executive. His understanding and appreciation of human differences weren't at all what I was expecting. So, in getting to know him—the *real* him—I asked, "Help me understand, Chris. How is it that you get it?" Settling back in his chair, Chris took a deep breath and glanced out the window. I realized he didn't get this asked very often, but he told me his story:

I think I was around seven or eight years old—old enough to be aware of the world around me, but maybe not old enough to make total sense of it. I will never forget a day when my father and I were walking down a sidewalk. This happened in the Deep South of the United States. Even though we were within a stone's throw of the civil rights movement, I had no idea what that conversation really was about. I saw an old Black man approaching, moving toward us on the sidewalk, walking in the opposite direction. He must have been in his seventies. Just when we reached a place where someone would have to turn to avoid bumping into each other, this old man stepped off the sidewalk and into the street. He just casually did this rather than trying to finagle himself around my father or me.

Chris paused, and sighed at the memory, still fresh in his mind. He looked down at the floor for a moment before continuing:

I was as surprised and curious as an eight-year-old boy could be. When I was growing up, children were not acknowledged or heard unless given permission to speak. Yet, this grown, elderly man stepped off the curb for me. Not only that, there was something about this old man's attitude that was almost reverent. There was something in the purposeful way he had moved to the street, to allow space for this white boy to continue walking, that impacted me deeply. I wasn't sure what had happened, but it was significant. I've always remembered this old man, and how that day has made me feel for years after that moment.

He went on to share that he often reflected on the incident, reminiscing on it almost as a "coming of age" event. That moment had an impact on who he was and how he thought about human differences for many years after that:

> Only as I got older, I wondered, why would an adult open up the space for me, as a kid, to continue walking, while he moved to the side? That's how I got it. The moment I realized how an elderly Black man was made to feel in the presence of a white boy. That's when I knew something was just wrong.

At that time, there was no training he'd attended, no coach, no business article to review, but as a young child, a certain perspective started to take shape. It was a real, unscripted, unguarded, unanticipated event that *just happened*. But what if he had never had this or another similar experience? Would he have still become a leader who gets it?

It's not possible to know for sure, but something in his mind was opened, primed, and ready to reach a deeper understanding of the world around him—just as it can happen to you now, as you start reading this book. We are all potentially ready to get it, if we pay attention. The opportunity to learn and understand others who are not like you comes your way every single day. You just have to look for it because, like Chris, it may be as small as someone's reaction to your presence, or comment, or conversation.

Chris's story was only one of the many stories and experiences I've encountered in working for more than two decades with people around the world. There are many other stories of leaders who could identify a past experience, a conversation, an observation, a moment in time in which they felt something was just not right.

Knowing that D&I is so human, so personal, so real, I decided the best way to guide you to greater leadership impact was to write a business memoir rather than a business manual. I decided to share the stories and awakenings of others that would encourage you to seek or rediscover your own experiences and insights, those you may have been missing or ignoring, until now.

I also realize that, even if you're compelled and inspired by learning from the stories and experiences of others, you may still want to have something like a "D&I manual." You may be looking for someone to break down a process on how to address diversity and inclusion. You may be seeking a step-by-step guide you can memorize, to act on to create change, but getting it doesn't really begin that way at all. There's often no rhyme or reason to what catches our attention. But I can assure you that once you spend more time discovering and understanding the life experiences you may have missed or ignored, you will exponentially increase your ability to understand and actually use the D&I guidance and recommendations available to you.

THE 5 DUALITIES OF
DIVERSITY AND INCLUSION

Part One of this book is about finding identity in your diversity. For the same reason I told you about Chris, it's important that you, as an individual, as a leader, develop a deep sense of your own identity. Why do you think the way you do? What is your place in relation to others who are not like you? How do you place value or pass judgment about the human differences around you? I encourage you to start thinking about those things. This is about your own story and the moments that helped you get it, or the process of seeking those moments you may have not yet experienced. To engage with authenticity in this topic, I started this book with my own moments of getting it.

Part Two unpacks the five dualities I discovered when digging deeper in the way we think about and manage diversity and inclusion in the work environment. In this section, you will learn the following:

- The rationale and understanding of each D&I duality, so you can use them as guideposts of what defines you as a leader, a professional, a human being.

- The stories and examples of how each of the D&I dualities plays out in real life and work situations.

- The research you can use as reference to further expand on the topics I'm sharing with you in this book.

As you learn about the five dualities of D&I, keep in mind **what they are** and **what they are not:**

- **The dualities are mindsets and practical leadership behaviors** that will take you from the *intent* to understand and leverage human differences, to having the most positive *impact* in understanding and engaging others who are different from you. The five dualities of diversity and inclusion are complementary to each other. I didn't learn about or test their practical application all at once. They revealed themselves piece by piece, example by example. I would go through my daily work on D&I, addressing different situations, where we needed to understand and reconcile diverse perspectives before making decisions. I would analyze and research the behaviors that explained the outcomes in each of those decisions. This gave me moments of self-discovery, a point where a duality of behaviors was revealed. But sometimes I was unable to figure out if there was a pattern that could explain those behaviors or not. Those were the times I had to set aside those experiences, and what I had learned from them, until I found a different piece of what started to look like a puzzle. It took me almost eight years to put the puzzle together—the five dualities of diversity and inclusion—and then start writing this book. So be patient and kind to yourself. It's not a race. It's a quest.

14

- **The dualities are not paradoxes.** For each duality, I will share with you practices and behaviors that may seem to be in contradiction or opposition, until you realize how they actually complement each other. You should not position yourself in one *or* the other side of each duality, like you would do with a personality assessment. The components of each duality are a fluid range of behaviors we all practice and experience every single day, without necessarily being deeply conscious about their origin, or how they impact the way you relate to others you see as different from you. They are a continuum, with a slider that moves day by day. Some days you may be farther left on the continuum, others you may be farther right. It's a process. Learn to flow, and adapt as you learn. The goal is to gain awareness, practice and growth that leads to greater impact.

You may think about the five dualities as five parts of your brain, and the function they play in how you perceive the world around you:

- **Duality 1: Connect and Learn** is the core, the base where the other four dualities sit. It's like the cerebellum, the part of the brain that controls our motor functions and makes us stay upright. Connect and Learn helps you maintain a mental, psychological, and emotional balance. On D&I, you seek a balance between your similarities and your differences from other people.

- **Duality 2**: **Think and Know** is like the frontal lobe, which makes up two-thirds of the brain. It is vital for memory, attention, motivation, and numerous other daily tasks. Think and Know is the duality that helps you solve problems and make judgments between what you think (based on observations or assumptions), and what you know (based on verified conclusions).

- **Duality 3: Pain and Possibility** is like the parietal lobe, that controls your body orientation (left and right) and your sensations. The parietal lobe also plays an important role in integrating sensory information from various parts of the body. It controls the sensory awareness of our physical body. On D&I, you may lead in a way that avoids the painful sensation of conflict, but also consider the positive impact of possibilities in your work environment.

- **Duality 4: Risk and Invest** is like the occipital lobe, the visual processing center. It controls vision, what we see, and how we see it. In diversity and inclusion, there are opportunities to lead with a vision that minimizes your risks, but also maximizes your investments.

- **Duality 5: Perform and Innovate** is like the temporal lobe, that controls hearing and behavior. You can move from hearing about diversity as noise that slows down your performance, to leading with inclusive behaviors that truly spark innovation.

Part Three of this book is a call to action. It's the encouragement to maximize your impact, own your choices and make decisions that can lead to an expedited evolution or an accelerated revolution on diversity and inclusion. The appendix includes tools you can use to apply the concepts and recommendations on each of the D&I dualities.

It is my hope that this book will give you the depth of understanding you may be seeking to set your own path forward: to move from your best *intent* to your most unprecedented *impact* in understanding, valuing and leveraging human differences.

PART ONE

FINDING YOUR IDENTITY
IN DIVERSITY

"The willingness to reach inside every part of
yourself opens the door to total understanding...
When you hold some part of yourself in reserve
you deny it exposure to life; you repress its energy and
keep it from understanding what it needs to know."[1]
—Deepak Chopra

We can certainly find inspiration and derive curiosity from the stories and experiences of others. But if you want to be a leader who gets it, you must seek, discover, and dwell on your personal experiences. These are the experiences that will help you see what you may have been missing. You need to feel, think, reflect on, and sometimes become vulnerable enough to incorporate that experience into your character. Yes, it means you have to "get real." These experiences—unexpected, unscripted, and powerful—raise you to a level of understanding that is different from constructs created with previous mindsets, with different social, political and economic purposes.

When rediscovering yourself and others, you may sometimes break into that emotional ugly cry that happens when we're deeply upset or moved. You know, the cry where your nose and your eyes swell up, when you feel like a five-year-old child when someone just broke your favorite toy. Or you may reach an intellectually guarded place where you feel foolish, betrayed, incompetent, or ashamed, thinking that you "just didn't know"—and you now realize it.

If it helps at all, let me assure you this happens to everyone: people of color, white people, women, men, the middle-aged and elderly, teenagers and kids. If we're lucky, we learn it young. But no matter how old you are, it is never too late to get it.

You may be meek or compliant, angry or frustrated, arrogant or oblivious of how you come across to others. This has an impact on others just as their moods impact you. That's what I urge you to consider, to look inward first, so you can then expand your level of awareness, understanding of, and impact on other human beings.

My intent is not to convince you to change who you are or what you believe as part of your process to get it. That is something only you can decide on. But I do want to share a very powerful lesson: the best thing you can do to address diversity and inclusion is to open your mind to other points of view, to new knowledge and a different way of understanding.

New approaches may crack open or even shatter fixed ideas you've had about people who are different from you. My expectation is that you'll feel compelled to seek experiences you may have been missing, or reinterpret those you already had, to recognize the lesson in them. That is the way to wake up, see, hear, feel, and learn. Remember that lesson throughout this book. It matters.

CHAPTER 1

HOW IT STARTED

"Don't worry. You're going to love it." My mother's words kept coming back to me as the state line crept closer. It was Saturday, February 2, 2002, and I was on a four-hour flight from my home in Puerto Rico to my new home—at least for the time being—in New Jersey. A heavy snowstorm was blasting through the East Coast, making travel a challenge. On the ground again, and on my way to what would be my temporary apartment, the view through the car's windshield was like the iconic scene in *Star Wars:* rapid white lines of snow smashed unrelentingly onto the glass, before dissolving into the night.

This trip was the beginning of my relocation process. I was headed to an exciting new job at my employer's company headquarters. Just after September 11, 2001, moving anywhere near Ground Zero was a bit scary. However, I had worked for this organization for almost five years and was ready to take on a new opportunity. As I pulled up to my new residence, I could still hear the *Star Wars* theme in my head: "Dah dah, dah dah dah DAAAH, dah" ... over and over again.

Thinking back on that flight, I remember feeling a quiet yet nervous rush of excitement washing over me. This move meant I was leaving behind the life I had known in Puerto Rico, coming to a new environment, away from the family and friends I loved. I realized that moving to a new place would also mean I'd have to think how to create some new daily routines. Yet, throughout those early days in my new world, the words of my mother kept coming back to tell me: "Don't worry. You're going to love it."

I trusted those words. They were comforting to me. I could lean on them. My mother's love for me and confidence in me was something I could tap into even though I was far away from her now.

As I stepped out of the car and stood in front of my new home, I started my usual process of trying to anticipate any potential challenges *before* they could become big problems. The first one ahead was the relentless snowfall. I took to figuring out when would be the right time to start shoveling the incessant waves of snow that had already accumulated on the sidewalk. It was a simple task, yet one that would gradually become a metaphor for this new chapter of my life.

It was a decision that seemed so small, but as those familiar with snowy weather know well, it's something that needs to be handled quickly and thoroughly. There is no question that shoveling a few inches of snow over a few hours is much easier than moving a foot or more of it after it has accumulated. Similarly, in life, dealing with small and seemingly non-urgent issues at the right time can also make a difference over the long term. It isn't the big things that derail us. Rather, it's the steady accumulation of little things that become frozen, immovable challenges.

Yes, I like metaphors and analogies. They communicate so much with so little effort. In this new chapter of my life, metaphors would become a shorthand for recognizing and tackling challenges I never saw coming. It would be a metaphor that prompted me to write this book, to face my fears, to understand a new culture, and a new way of seeing the world.

I faced this job change with confidence and joy. What was to fear? After all, I was relocating within the same company. I would report to the same person I had reported to a few years before. I knew many of my colleagues. I was respected and valued by the organization. I was confident in my experience and ability to perform very well in my new role. Having grown up in a bilingual household, I didn't anticipate any particular language barriers either, so I thought: *Hey, this is going to be great! I'll need to figure out some things, and that's okay.* Finally, I've always loved the thrill and the challenge of being an explorer. So here I was, ready for the discovery.

That was almost two decades ago. That was the day my mission in D&I really started.

How did D&I become the choice I made after fifteen years working in Human Resources? It was a thing I did, because I wanted to keep moving forward in my career. I asked leaders at the organization where I was working, what they would recommend I focus on to further advance my career at the company. I had developed the habit of asking for this one piece of advice every time I was about to move to a new role. Most leaders felt very comfortable and even flattered to be asked. They consistently gave me focused, pertinent, honest, and helpful suggestions based on our time working with each other. One day, I was about to ask for that piece of advice— not realizing that it would change me in ways I didn't expect.

I had worked at this leader's organization for a few years, receiving outstanding performance reviews, having the opportunity to create new solutions, taking on challenging projects and leveraging every opportunity to further develop my skills, which also brought value to the company. Sitting in his office, enthusiastically waiting for his pearls of wisdom prior to my parting, I anticipated he would be brief and precise. Being a direct communicator, I knew he would be clear and specific in his recommendation, and when a very busy leader takes a few minutes to share the advice you request, you really feel privileged.

"…So, you want to know what to do to keep moving up?" he asked.

"Yes, absolutely!" I replied.

And looking at me with a quick glance, he said: "Well, don't get me wrong, but I would work on your accent."

For some time after this conversation, I tried to remember if he said anything else after that, but no, there was nothing else. He simply stated I should work on my accent. Needless to say, a few minutes after the "I was not expecting that" surprise moment, I felt lost. I had spent several years working hard and smart for this team, and my parting gift of wisdom had nothing to do with what I did for the organization. Rather, it had everything to do with who I was.

I could have focused on the hurt, or the confusion, but I took a step back. Yes, I felt a sting, I was disappointed and hurt. But more than anything, I needed to figure out how to *think* about this, and then what to do about it, so I did.

I realized I didn't sound like others in my department, but I knew, or assumed, I was always understood. No one had ever asked me to repeat what I said or anything like that. Trying to help me process what I was feeling, someone who had known that leader for many years, said to me: "He probably told you something others have thought as well, but wouldn't tell you. He appreciates you and wants you to be successful." This perspective helped me reframe my initial reaction, which was something I needed to do for myself. There was a lot to learn from that moment. It was a pivotal point in my life—the beginning of the journey that led me to write this book.

It took me a long time to come to terms with that leader's advice. Even if it was done with the best of intentions, I struggled to process his suggestions. I figured he *did* want me to be successful. He told me the one thing that stood out in his mind as something that might stand in my way of success—in *his* worldview and experience, something that other people may have been afraid to tell me. But I was conflicted.

I didn't want to allow my mind to go to the negative place where my emotions were leading it. I knew this leader, and something inside me said: "I have never perceived him as prejudiced against people like me. I really have not!" But was I being naïve? Was it that I was just discovering something I didn't realize before?

Maybe that leader could have clarified or added to his comment, but I didn't ask. He may have been able to give me examples, or explain why he believed my accent would impact my future career growth. He may have been able to point back at an incident in which he experienced my accent being a hindrance, but I didn't get to it. I was too stunned and disappointed to ask him.

I realized he truly gave me the pearl I was looking for, but more than the career advice I was expecting, his words became a hard lesson about how people think about people, voices, clothing, culture and things that are different from them. That moment taught me a lot about myself, about how offended I was when I felt that my identity was being diminished. I'm sure you may have a similar experience in your life, because these things can happen to everyone.

With time, I realized that I had missed two big opportunities that day:

- The opportunity **for me to learn** that this was not only about me, but something that impacts others as well.

- The opportunity **for him to learn** more about the conscious or unconscious thoughts that led him to that recommendation.

I missed the opportunity to have a courageous and enlightening conversation that would have made both of us better for it. I had a chance to ask myself how I could change the game while playing the game of business, of being who I am—the best version of who I am and who I could become.

I needed to figure out how to *share* myself without *selling* myself. It took pain, insight, and learning, all of which I am now sharing with you.

My intent is that you see reflections of yourself and your own possibilities in the experiences I have decided to share with you. Use them to look inside you and around you. Determine if there are still parts of yourself that are held in reserve, because one or more experiences created a conflict between your identity and your aspirations.

THE ETHNIC LABEL DILEMMA

What I didn't anticipate when I moved to the US was that I would always remember that four-hour flight headed north. I didn't realize it would change my life in so many ways. What I thought was an ordinary flight came with unanticipated meaning, and yes, a metaphor. I had departed San Juan as a human resources professional. Two days later, on the first day at my US office, I wasn't just a person with a role in an organization I loved. To my surprise I had now become an "ethnically diverse" person.

When I walked into my new office, I got a binder with onboarding materials, including one inviting me to become part of the company's Hispanic employee organization. *Ok, I'm Hispanic now!* was the first thought that crossed my mind. Don't get me wrong. Technically speaking, I knew what the word meant. What I didn't know was what it would come to mean to me personally. I was unaware of the lens through which people would see me, based on their

27

ideas of what a Hispanic was, is, or should be. What I came to learn was that instead of: "This is Monica, our HR person," even when people wouldn't actually say it, the way that sentence would sound like now was: "This is Monica, our Hispanic HR person."

I'd been one of very few female executives in a former leadership role. I knew how to operate in a male-dominated work environment, but this new Hispanic label was not one I was used to. In fact, for some time, it became quite uncomfortable to be branded in a way that I had not figured out what it meant for myself. Nonetheless, I was rather intrigued.

As you may already know, the term Hispanic refers to people with an ethnic background from Spanish-speaking countries. The US Census Bureau uses the term "Hispanic or Latino" to refer to "a person of Cuban, Mexican, Puerto Rican, South or Central American, or other (predominantly) Spanish-speaking culture, regardless of race."[2] That means Hispanics or Latinos can be of any race. We have Black Hispanics, white Hispanic, "cafe con leche" (another way of saying Brown) Hispanics, and so on. Because they can sometimes be used interchangeably, not everyone understands or makes the subtle distinction between the terms Hispanic and Latino.

Latino is the geographically specific reference to people from Latin America, including Brazil (where the predominant language is Portuguese). In other words, the term Latino encompasses a group of people from the "America" that is not the "US-America" or Canada. Not that Latinos chose to call themselves in a polarizing way: "all of us" versus "them." Rather, these terms were coined in the

US to refer to others who share cultural traditions (language or geography) that are of non-Anglo-Saxon heritage. In fact, amongst Hispanics/Latinos, we'd rather refer to ourselves according to our nationality, our country of heritage (*Yo soy de Puerto Rico*, or *Yo soy Puertorriqueña*).

Just to add a few more layers to the cultural discourse, there are many Hispanics who don't identify as Latinos, and Latinos who don't refer to themselves as Hispanic. Even more recently, the term Latinx has been used to provide a gender-neutral reference to the otherwise gender-specific terms of Latino (men) and Latina (women). Confused yet? Is your mind going in circles? No worries—welcome to the joys of building cultural fluency!

MY LATINA AWAKENING

I chose to get curious about the notion of thinking about myself as Hispanic, even more, as Latina. I took it on as a type of *identity* challenge.

Just as I'd never had to think about the appropriate time to shovel snow, I didn't know whether to deal with this challenge in increments or wait to see if it would build up in a way that would ultimately *demand* my attention. On a frequent basis I thought of ignoring the whole thing, and just focus on being *Mónica*. However, there was a contrarian concern in my mind.

I kept thinking that if I didn't address it at the appropriate time, it could become a big pile of snow that would require much heavier lifting. It could melt one day and refreeze the next. The risk was that, when it became more of an iceberg blocking my sidewalk, I wouldn't be able to just quickly shovel it away to move forward.

One day, I was on my way to a mid-morning meeting at my company's headquarters. As I walked down the hallway, I noticed the beauty of brightness coming through a skylight in the middle of the foyer. This magnificent flood of light stood in shining contrast to the rather dark and gloomy conference room I was about to enter.

As other colleagues walked in, something else caught my attention: They all looked more or less the same: somber, serious and even sad. At least, that is how it looked to me. They were all dressed in strict black or gray. I couldn't help thinking that the turquoise color of my blazer was way brighter than any piece of wardrobe, meeting materials, or furnishings in that room. As we waited for the meeting to begin, we made small talk and reacted to a few jokes that somebody made. That's when my colorful attire became a match to my laughter, which sounded louder than anyone else's in the room. Needless to say, I was feeling a little bit out of place, but that was still okay. I was confident in myself and knew I had a lot to contribute in the conversation.

Once the meeting started, I practiced the Catholic school habit of raising my hand to wait for a turn to speak. However, I noticed no one else was doing that. Other people seemed to have a highly developed conversation skill. They had the ability to determine when someone else was about to finish a sentence, and then jump in, like people merging from the on-ramp to the highway. There was an almost seamless transition in the conversation. No one was checking who had raised their hand, and for the most part, no other hands were raised. Only mine.

When it finally seemed that everyone else had expressed their opinion, I offered my thoughts on the topic being discussed. That was when I made the fourth most important observation of that day: the "eloquence" of my hands. I hadn't paid much attention to it before that day, but when I speak, my hands have the tendency to take on a life of their own in front of my face. That day in particular, my carefully manicured nails seemed to glow with the brightness of a Caribbean coral polish.

As the meeting got close to an end, I wondered if my words were a bit off that day, since I was not getting much of a reaction to my comments. I couldn't help thinking… Were all of my differences becoming a distraction from what I had to say?

At the end of the session, my observational mode wrapped up when somebody asked about the origin of my accent. To my surprise, I thought, *"Do I have an accent?"*

Don't get me wrong, I was not naïve about my intonation. What I learned that day was how much my wardrobe, my laughter, my hand gestures, my nail polish, and now my accent separated me from the norms that surrounded me.

After I left that meeting, I had to physically stop in the hallway, trying to figure out: *What does this all mean to me?* Over the next few months, I got similar questions and comments. Someone even said at one point that, for being Latina, I didn't really look like one. I felt confused! Was *who I am* getting in the way of what I wanted to do? Was it becoming a deterrent to my career aspirations? Even more than by virtue of my gender, was I reaching the proverbial glass ceiling due to my cultural identity?

I sensed that I had walked into and stood on a cultural landmine and I was waiting for it to go off—or not. What would I do now? Were these defining elements of who I am, or were there any other things that really defined me? Did I have to choose what or who I was? And why? Did I need to change who I was to maintain my career progression?

THE FIRST TIME YOU FELT DIFFERENT

As impactful as the *Latina awakening* was to me, it's important to recognize that almost at any time, and for a variety of reasons, everyone can feel they don't belong in their environment. Think about it and ask yourself:

- When was the first time *you felt different?*

- What was the *impact it had on you?*

- What did you *do or didn't do* about it?

People can feel different because of their age, race, height, body build, weight, good looks or bad looks, background, personality, financial status, the car they drive, the neighborhood they live in, and whether they rent or own their housing. Teenagers might bully others who don't wear the right sneakers, or whose pants are not high enough, low enough, tight enough, or loose enough.

Therefore, some might argue that a Latina speaking about belonging is not different than how everybody else can feel at any particular time. Because we can all feel different from others in more than one way and understand how uncomfortable or disenfranchising this can be, some may think this becomes an "equalizer" that makes the discussion about diversity and inclusion an irrelevant one. For example: I had a colleague who looked like a fashion model, always thoughtful about how he looked. You would have thought he was a movie star visiting our company, but he was actually a computer whiz. He looked (and felt) quite different from others who took pride in fitting the stereotype of a "geek," which by the way, can be a true compliment in the world of technology.

So, let's be real. Some may think that people should "look above our differences," or more bluntly said, "get over it," blend in, look for the commonalities and minimize our differences. I understand the merits and intent behind that thought, which is why I will discuss it in greater detail in Chapter 3. At this point, I ask that you consider five important elements on the impact of our differences: *meaning, value, identity, prevalence,* and *choice.*

Think about the ways you see or feel different from those around you and ask yourself the following questions:

- What does that difference **mean** to you?
- How much **value** does that difference have to you?
- How much is that difference part of what you consider to be your true *identity?*
- How **prevalent** or omnipresent is that difference in your daily life?

- Do you even have the **choice** to change that difference if you wanted to?

The answer you give to these questions is what distinguishes the impact your differences have in how you experience life—personally, socially, and at work.

Those who have childhood experiences of being bullied, of feeling "less than" others, develop a long-lasting mental impression of that experience. They will remember details of it, who took part in it, and how they felt about it well into adulthood.

If as a child you felt different because of your weight, your thick eyeglasses, your speech impediment, the low quality of your clothing, your crooked teeth, or your nerdy IQ, you know what that feels like. You may have also experienced a very different reality at a later time, if or when you changed your eating habits, got contact lenses, took speech therapy, gained financial strength to purchase brand-name attire, got braces, or suddenly became regarded as a trendy geek.

Now, imagine the impact of being different in ways that you *cannot* change. Even if not the same, your early experience can help you consider the impact on those who are and feel different throughout their whole lives, because of the color of their skin, their sexual orientation, their disability, and many more.

❝ Not all differences are created equal.
Not all have the same implications.
**Some differences last a season. Some last a lifetime. **

34

THE "A" WORDS

My Latina awakening was a moment of truth, when the differences I was discovering, and the ones I still had to uncover, contributed to the feeling that somehow, I didn't belong in the environment where I so much wanted to fit in. I couldn't ignore the reality that was in front of me. As Kenji Yoshino eloquently describes in his writings, I had to decide if this was the time to "convert, pass, or cover" my differences.[3] This was a painful task to accomplish. I could choose to change the colors of my wardrobe, tone down my laughter, make my hands "mute" and go for a "pink and white" manicure. I could, and for some time, and in specific instances, I actually did.

While I still felt I was giving away part of myself, I could reasonably adapt in that way. Shifting the attention from my colorful ensemble to a greater focus on the ideas I wanted to share was a worthy tradeoff.

But I kept asking myself, *where does it stop?* I could have taken accent reduction lessons, made my communication less conversational and talked in bullet point fashion. I could decide to drop my maiden name for my married name, or change its pronunciation to "Maneca Dyas," instead of Mónica Díaz—I could, but I did not. That's where I drew a line, when it came to the decision of how to pronounce my own name. Maybe I would have made a different decision if my name was too long, but that was not the case. I had to think, to figure out which elements had a deeper meaning to me, which ones defined who I am: my heritage, my personality, and my identity. Those could not be compromised in achieving what I wanted to do.

Adapt what is useful, reject what is useless,
and add what is specifically your own.
—Bruce Lee

When we say that change is constant, we're not only referring to external forces or events happening *to* us or *around* us. We're referring to our internal processes as well. Our mind, our boundaries, our preferences, beliefs—they're always changing based on events, people, reflections, and our personal awareness and growth. The important thing to remember is that we have a choice. We can reframe the event and look for the silver lining, the potential, the opportunity in those events, or we can succumb to them, seeing them as the inevitable result of being different.

I am referring to changes happening within us as well as outside of us. A new environment, a new reality, will require that you adapt or rise above your circumstances. You adapt or succumb, because at a more profound level, the feeling that you don't belong could consume you—as a child in the playground, a professional in a business setting or an elderly employee whose connections start diminishing as time goes by.[4] Or you can look for the opportunities and advantages you can seize in the moment.

As you adapt to a new environment, be mindful of the range of differences you choose to change or not, so you don't end up losing perspective of who you truly are. One of the things that stands out about many people who have risen beyond their differences is the fact they were able to find, create, or act on the opportunities they found in those circumstances.

When I speak about the personal and cultural tradeoffs I made as my career developed, some people praise my "professional career commitment," while others can be critical of "the need to assimilate." This is not something I take lightly, because for the most part, each of those tradeoffs were conscious decisions I had to think about at every step of the way, because there are important differences between *assimilation*, *acculturation* and *affirmation*. They are all ways of adapting to our surroundings, yet carry different weight in how you think about our own identity. For example:

- **Assimilation** is a concept most commonly used in anthropology and sociology. It refers to the process where individuals or groups of differing ethnic heritage are *absorbed* or *integrated* into a dominant culture or society. Assimilation implies that a group of people take the traits of a dominant culture to such a degree that the assimilating group becomes socially indistinguishable from other members of the society.

  Although assimilation may be compelled through force or undertaken voluntarily, it's rare for a minority group to replace its previous cultural practices completely; religion, food preferences, proxemics (the physical distance between people in a given social situation), and aesthetics are among the characteristics that tend to be most resistant to change.[5]

- **Acculturation** is a process of social, psychological, and cultural change that stems from *balancing two cultures* while adapting to the prevailing culture of the society. Although there are multiple variations and levels of this definition,[6] acculturation implies that individuals adjust to a new environment, by adopting or participating in aspects of the more prevalent culture, without losing or rejecting their culture of origin.

- **Affirmation** is less commonly referenced in the same sociological framework as the concepts of assimilation and acculturation. However, affirmations adequately explain the decisions or formal *declarations* we make to ourselves, and to others, in the process of adapting to a new culture. Displaying the flag of our country of origin is an affirmation. Choosing to start our greetings in our native language is an affirmation. Wearing artifacts that reveal our ancestry or religious affiliation is an affirmation. Such affirmations are, for the most part, conscious decisions that acknowledge and communicate the values and tenets of our identity that we don't want to cover or change. On the contrary, they are choices we make on how we define ourselves and what we want others to know and understand about us.

CHOICES OF AFFIRMATION

The dilemma of assimilation, acculturation, or affirmation was not something I fully understood during my Latina awakening. I didn't know if the cultural differences that challenged me would disappear with time or if they would be ever-present as part of my new reality, so I went back to my explorer/researcher mode. I decided to "run a few single-blind studies" to determine the impact of intentionally changing cultural variables in my daily delivery.[7] Since I was the only one who knew what I was researching, I felt safe in my exploration. No matter what happened, there was no risk of public failure. The findings of my research would only be recorded in my head, until now, that I'm telling you the story.

I was about to deliver a presentation in one of those dark and gloomy conference rooms adjacent to the light-flooded foyer at my company's headquarters. I had prepared my presentation with the usual attention to detail: I was well versed on the topic; had practiced my talking points, introductory stories, segues, and the key takeaways of my message; had analyzed and verified all the supporting data; had ensured there were no typos on the materials; had prepared summary handouts; and was ready for any technology glitches or questions that my audience might have.

Yes, it was business as usual. This time, though, I was also conducting my personal/cultural experiment, with a few controlled variables: my usually "very joyful" demeanor, the color palette of my wardrobe and nail polish, as well as the "activation of my talking hands."

I was wearing a black skirt and a gray top—nothing flashy. My nails were polished in a French manicure and I practiced holding my hands close to my torso in a "self-handshake" mode. I made the conscious choice to smile less frequently during my presentation, projecting a more reflective demeanor. Above all this, I was also determined to make this an enjoyable experience, instead of getting too much into my own head. Playing with each control variable, I observed the reactions at every step of my delivery. Yes, I had fun with it, however I must also say this was not easy to do.

There were a lot of elements to remember, while I still needed to focus on the content of my presentation. I kept asking myself, *does every professional have to go through all this? Is it because I'm a woman that I have to make all these adjustments to present to an audience that is mostly men? Is it because I'm Latina that I have to learn how to be less like me and more like them? Or is it just because I want to further advance my career and be successful?* Yes… I kept trying not to be too much into my head.

From a knowledge and expertise level, this presentation was no different from the ones I had delivered a few months earlier. However, this time, I was able to successfully manage every variable of my experiment. I felt good about it. As my presentation came to a close and people started to leave, I saw my boss slowly approach the front of the room, where I was still standing. He looked at me with a concealed smile. Almost as a whisper, he said: "This is the most professionally polished presentation I've ever seen you give."

The movie froze at that point. I was immediately pleased by the compliment. I took the success I had created and gave myself a pat in the back for it. Now it was time to record and analyze the results of my experiment, to come up with a conclusion. Part of me wanted to be very positive, thinking that great speakers truly have to master their storytelling and their delivery, and that's what I was doing. I was adapting. I was learning. I was in control of myself. But part of me couldn't help thinking about "innovators and disruptors," who don't conform to the norms. They change every known model of doing what they do, creating transformation as they go.

For some reason, I kept thinking about the 1998 movie *Patch Adams,* where Robin Williams portrayed Hunter Doherty "Patch" Adams, a physician who believes that play is part of healing, although this concept contradicted what was acceptable medical practice. Some people, like Dr. Adams, and other colorful leaders we all know, get away with their differences. They embrace their oddities, and most of those around them accept them, or at least tolerate them. They have the freedom to be themselves, even if they have to fight for it every day. They seem to find their balance and rest there. Some find this balance naturally; some evolve into it. So, I asked myself:

- How much do I want to give away in order to achieve my career aspirations?

- Do I have to "sell myself," look and sound like someone else to be successful?

- Who do I want to be? The one who adapts to succeed or the one who disrupts to transform?

It took me a while to understand that it was not about changing myself. It was about *creating* myself, about *evolving* my own self, about *becoming a better version* of myself. The most important thing was that, at every step of the way, I had to *know* and *feel* that it was *my* choice, not anyone else's choice. As long as I was clear on what I was deciding and why, I would be ok. I would still be myself. I could decide to adapt to my audience when I was presenting, as long as I was still comfortable in my own skin. If I could adapt my delivery in a way that increased the attention to my message, then I wanted that. Still, it was important to find ways to reach that balance between who I was and who I wanted to be, while being me. I had to decide which were the differences that would become my affirmations.

"I do know one thing about me:
I don't measure myself by others' expectations
or let others define my worth."[8]
—Sonia Sotomayor

For some time, I observed how some people use their differences to their advantage and thought: Which were the ones I would want to affirm for myself, even if it may not be too advantageous? Would I still want to do this even if others could still think (and not tell me) these might hinder my career progression? That would become the balance between **what I adapted to succeed** and **what I disrupted to transform**.

Marketing and branding professionals would tell their clients to think about the unique attributes of their products. Those unique attributes, properly showcased and nurtured, are what makes a brand or company stand out from their competitors. It's also how a brand is developed and strengthened. And what is a brand? It's the image people get in their minds, or the feeling they have when they hear the name of the company. So I wondered, why not use what makes me different to positively "differentiate" myself? To stand out for what is unique in me? Why not? I could do that, so I did. My affirmations then became easier to declare:

- **Color.** I chose color, which gives me energy and exudes energy. My *Latinidad* is expressed in vivid color, in how I dress, the materials I use to present content to an audience, and the color of the seats in my car! I would care less if the expression of color triggers a stereotypical perception in others. That is my space of affirmation and I celebrate it.

- **Accent.** I chose my accent. I would not conceal it or "work" on it. I would acknowledge it, because it reminds me where I come from and connects me with my culture. I want to still recognize there is a Latina in my words, as much as in my heart.

- **Expression.** Although I may be a bit louder or more energetic than others, I embrace it. It's my way of celebrating life and living my life. I can adjust my tone when necessary or appropriate, yet being an expressive Latina is my true self.

Do you remember your awakening?
Have you declared the affirmations of your identity?

Declaring my own cultural affirmations was a process of discovery that didn't happen in isolation. As anything in life, when you're deeply immersed in a situation, it's a lot easier for others standing from a distance to see the forest, not only the trees. With some initial hesitation and an abundance of humility, I shared my Latina awakening dilemmas with a few mentors, and later on, with an executive coach. To this day, I'm grateful for the immeasurable value of their advice.

Lessons Learned

- **Know what makes you great**. Figure out your most salient strengths, the ones you recognize in yourself and the ones others recognize in you. Balance your safer space of introspection with your potential vulnerability to the perspective of others.

- **Let your differences become your differentiator**. It's *your* choice. What are the differences that really define you, the ones that have a deeper meaning to you? There are no good or bad decisions, only *your* choices. Your cultural affirmations are as important as what you know and the work you do. The right opportunities for you are the ones where those elements are not in conflict.

- **Don't "sell" yourself, share yourself**. Acknowledge who you are in front of others. Don't think you have to sell yourself as you adapt to a new environment. Once you have determined which are your affirmations, share them with others, even if you may think they can become a bit controversial. This is the space where leadership and personal authenticity begins. Your authenticity as a leader will show others that they can authentically be themselves in front of you as well.

CAREER CROSSROADS

Just a couple of years after that four-hour flight headed north, I was still processing my thoughts about my Latina identity. I now faced a different dilemma: a *career* crossroad. I was considering accepting a diversity and inclusion role within the organization. This basically meant deviating from the human resources business partner career path I had been in for over a decade. Instead, this move would take me to a specialty role that didn't seem to carry the gravitas (at least then) of my current career trajectory.

After some consideration, I decided to meet with my manager and discuss it with him. I valued his sound judgment. His advice had always been very useful to me. As I explained my intent to make this change, I described how it would connect my professional experience in Human Resources with the more personal experience of working in a new environment, where cultural differences became part of what I needed to figure out to continue being successful. After listening for a few minutes, he looked at me with a hint of concern and gently asked: "Are you sure you want to do this? You may not be able to come back to your current career path if you do."

I know most people can relate to similar experiences. Someone tells you that you're about to leave a safe port, without the probability of returning if your trip doesn't go well. This realization can stop you in your tracks for a moment. You're moving in a direction that is different from what others expect of you. You're letting go of what you know and opening up a whole new space in front of you—a space that has no guarantees of success. You may not be completely sure how things will work out, or if they will work out at all. But in the words of Master Yoda, from *Star Wars,* this is a moment of *"Do or do not. There is no try."*

"Do or do not," happens when you're at the point where emotional and mental attachments untie to free you up. You know, in your gut, that the only way you can go is *forward.* A time like this can be quite scary, but making this kind of decision can also bring a liberating smile to your face. You know you're living your authentic life, when you experience exhilaration and joy that goes from an accelerated heartbeat to a deep sense of calmness. It's the same feeling I have now, as I write this book.

It's been quite a long time now, since I made the choice to take my career in a different direction, to specialize my work in diversity and inclusion. This professional journey granted me the opportunity to work in different industries, live in a variety of geographies, and meet a whole kaleidoscope of people from all around the world. Immersing myself in those experiences has continuously fed a curiosity about human differences.

I've enjoyed the discovery, but I've also felt the frustration of not seeing this work advance as much as some organizations declare they want to see it succeed. The insights developed while working with and seeking to understand the power of differences became the cornerstones of this book. Writing the book started as an idea that slowly became a necessity—to share with you the continuous practice of "learning and unlearning", to better understand others —your employees, your colleagues, your team—which, in turn, will help you become a better version of yourself.

CHAPTER 2
THINKING DIFFERENTLY

INNOVATORS AND DISRUPTORS

At age seventeen, Everette Taylor became one of the hundreds of thousands homeless people in the US. Rather than hide the fact that he was homeless, Taylor uses his experience to inspire others going through tough times. In an interview with *Inc.*, he shared how his experience of living in his car and being homeless gave him a whole new perspective on life—and how he became an entrepreneur.[9]

"Experiences like that teach you how to stand in another person's shoes," Taylor explained. "There's nothing better than being able to understand people." Taylor became the chief marketing officer at Skurt, a mobile app that lets you rent a car and have it delivered to you where you are.[10]

Colonel Harlan Sanders was a failure at everything most of his life—at least according to him. At age sixty-five, all he had to his name was a car, a chicken recipe, and his monthly $105 Social Security check. Nonetheless, he hit the road with the intent of selling his franchise idea anyway. He focused on what he had, but even more importantly *on what he wanted*, on the *impact* he wanted to achieve.[11] More than 1,000 (1,009 to be exact) restaurants rejected him before one finally accepted his offer. He had held to his vision of what was possible. He put action to his intent and the rest is history at Kentucky Fried Chicken.

We often think of Hillary Clinton as the first woman to seek the Democratic presidential nomination. But in 1972, while Clinton was still in law school, Patsy Mink became the first Asian-American woman to seek the Democratic presidential nomination.[12] Before entering politics, Mink aspired to be a doctor, but wasn't admitted to any of the colleges she applied to. She turned to law school instead, attending the University of Chicago School of Law. Mink would become the first woman of color elected to the US House of Representatives and the first Asian-American woman to serve in Congress. In addition to writing bills like Title IX, the Early Childhood Education Act, and the Women's Educational Equity Act, Mink was the first Asian-American to run for US president.

When Frederick Hutson was arrested for drug trafficking back in 2005, his future might have been one that reflected the US Sentencing Commission's research: that 49.3 percent of those arrested for federal offenses, including the 11.5 percent involved in drug trafficking, become repeat offenders. Hutson used his time in prison to launch Pigeonly, an application that provides a host of services to keep open lines of communication between inmates and their families. Only five years after launching Pigeonly, the app is one of the largest apps on the market, for connecting inmates and their families. It caters to inmates and their families across eighty-eight different countries worldwide.[13]

"A lot of times a thing that can be perceived as a weakness actually turn into the greatest strength and for me it was that," he said in an interview with *Forbes* magazine.[14] "It actually became the reason why people invested—because I've been there, and I know and understand this market better than anybody else."

Then there is J. K. Rowling, a single mother living on welfare, almost homeless, trying to support her daughter, who spent seven years writing her first Harry Potter book—much of that time on the train or in coffee shops. She didn't have an office and barely had an apartment. She submitted it to twelve major publishing houses, who all rejected the book. Today, she has an estimated worth of more than $1 billion—more than twice that of Steven King's estimated $400 million net worth.[15] What do you think she was telling herself about feeling overwhelmed, being a failure, and a nearly homeless woman before she found a publisher? Her focus was on the beautiful story she was creating. She moved from her intent—to inspire children to imagine a world of magic and empowerment—to the impact of a better, kinder world where all children have the chance to become leaders.

There are hundreds of rags-to-riches, failure-to-success stories. There are hundreds of how-to-books and memoirs that various successful people have written with details of how *they* did it. These are the *innovators*, who change or improve what already exists to make it better. These are also the *disruptors*, who break away in their industry or create new business ideas all together.

Many of these stories are of entrepreneurs who built business empires out of almost nothing, but don't you wonder about the stories of those who spark or lead innovation within existing organizations? Where are those stories? Who are those people? They most likely represent the majority of us—working for an organization, not creating it or owning it. Knowing more about these 'business protagonists' can help others realize they can be innovators and disruptors within their work environment as well. Following are a few examples:

Olga D. González-Sanabria is Hispanic.[16] Born in Puerto Rico, she received a bachelor of science degree from the University of Puerto Rico and a master of science degree from the University of Toledo, both in chemical engineering. As director of engineering at NASA's Glenn Research Center in Ohio, she is best known for her contributions to the development of long-life nickel hydrogen batteries that help power the International Space Station. If people think less of her for her nail color, or her accent, I doubt they say anything or that she worries about it much.

Dr. Ann Tsukamoto, a scientist, inventor, and stem cell researcher was among the scientists whose work in the 1990s helped discover human blood stem cells.[17] She went on to create the methodology to isolate them. Her co-patented invention was ground-breaking in creating advances in blood cancer treatment. She holds over a dozen patents, and has dedicated her life and work to using science to improve the life and health of others.

Dr. Shirley Jackson, a physicist, is the first African American woman to earn her doctorate at MIT in any field.[18] Her impressive accomplishments include working as theoretical physicist at Bell Laboratories and chairing the US Nuclear Regulatory Commission. Jackson's groundbreaking scientific research paved the way for numerous telecommunication inventions, including the touch-tone telephone, fiber optic cables, solar cells, the portable fax, and innovative technology that led to the development of caller ID and call-waiting.

Richard Montañez was born in Mexico and grew up picking grapes with his family in a small town in California.[19] Without a high school diploma, he got a job as a janitor at the Frito-Lay Rancho Cucamonga plant. Although Montañez had modest ambitions, he went to task after seeing a video where the president of the company asked employees to "act like an owner." After a machine broke in the assembly line, causing some Cheetos to not get dusted with the bright orange cheese powder the brand is famous for, Montañez took some home. Inspired by a Mexican *elote* (corncob), he thought of a spicier version that added "chili to Cheetos" and created his own recipe for it. With a borrowed marketing-strategy book and a $3 tie (his first ever), he put his new brand of Cheetos in sample bags that he designed himself and presented them to the company's president. The rest is a (profitable) history of Flamin' Hot Cheetos, Frito-Lay's top-selling snack. After forty-two years at the company, Montañez recently retired from PepsiCo, after being the executive vice president of multicultural sales and community activation for the North American divisions. He is now starting a new career chapter, leading his own innovation business.

For every one of the stories above, there are so many more that we don't know about—stories of people with diverse perspectives and backgrounds who found paths to creativity and innovation. Not all of them followed a rigorous scientific method (Montañez described his "PhD" as being "Poor, hungry, and Determined"). Their commonality is that they all saw and acted on an intersection of knowledge that had not been explored before. There is no question that each one of these people started with a focused intent, but then took one step after another to attain an impact that went far beyond their own initial expectations. This should be what every leader wants in an organization. So, how can you spark innovation and disruption? What is getting in your way?

As Adam Grant postulates in his book *Originals*, many organizations tend to suffocate the unorthodox views of people who think differently.[20] And when we say "think differently," you may be asking yourself, "What are we talking about? What do those different ideas look like?" These ideas may look or sound like the following:

- The objections of people who seem to have a "natural disposition" to contradict any idea you have.

- The thoughts of a few "IQ geniuses" that seem to exist in a different dimension on almost every topic.

- The perspectives of what you may call "critical thinkers" within your group.

- The rather infrequent or rhetorical question (not yet an idea) that someone may pose in a meeting.

- The ideas that remain silent, when people don't share them with you, thinking they don't have a chance of being considered.

We are talking about all of the above—the ideas that would probably take a conversation in a different direction if you let it. These are the ideas that may not align with your own thinking or preferences. In the absence of these ideas, you limit yourself to only hearing enhancements or build-ups on ideas you already had. Even worse, you may mostly hear the perspective of people who feel uber-confident that you will listen to *any* idea they have, different or not, just because it comes from them.

Lessons Learned

- Your goal should be to create an environment where different perspectives are shared, listened to and heard.

- Keep in mind there is a big distinction between the two: you hear with your ears, but you listen with your mind. The same way seeds grow stronger with good soil, water and sunshine, different perspectives will flourish in an inclusive work environment, where people's ideas are not only heard, but listened to.

DIFFERENCES THAT MATTER

So, you may be asking yourself, what is the best approach to unleash the power of our differences and foster innovation? How do you create that kind of environment?

Frans Johansson, author of *The Medici Effect,* is a strong proponent of how diversity and inclusion drive *intersectional innovation,* which is defined as the combination of ideas from different fields, increasing the chances of an *unusual* combination to occur.[21] In practice, such "intersections" can be generated by bringing together diverse people with different and diverse backgrounds, life experiences and perspectives, on a broad range of human dimensions. But over the past few years, how we define that "broad range of human dimensions" has been the subject of debate.

In some instances, business leaders and D&I colleagues have shifted the D&I narrative, from the focus on backgrounds and life experiences to what is known as **diversity of thought**.[22] As some of these leaders, you may be asking yourself which one is more important:

- **Differences of background and experience**: the most commonly recognized elements of diversity, such as race, ethnicity, gender, sexual orientation, disability, generational, religion, culture, and so on.

- **Differences in personality:** people's preferences, motive and ways of thinking, which is what *diversity of thought* refers to.

Which one should be the premise of your company's D&I strategy and efforts? Should you decide on one over the other? And, frankly speaking, is your decision based on sociopolitical concerns or an actual conviction of what is best for your organization?

As you keep reading this book, you will know more about my perspective on this topic from both a professional and personal perspective. You will see it unfold in the five dualities of diversity and inclusion I have coined for you. But let me summarize that perspective right upfront: As with many things in life, I'm convinced that the answer to this question should not be a matter of "this *or* that," but rather of "this *and* that." It's not a paradox, it's a duality. Let me explain.

As someone with an industrial/organizational psychology background, I wholeheartedly agree that understanding personality styles and preferences is important. They provide you information on **cognitive** differences.[23] These differences are related to our mental functions, such as learning, reasoning, perception and decision making. That is the reason tests and inventories, such as Myers-Briggs Type Indicator,[24] DISC,[25] Insights,[26] and Strengths Finder[27] continue being so popular in business environments. You may have taken many of these assessments before, in your executive hiring process, or as part of a team or leadership development program within your company. As long as you're looking to bring together different personality traits, these assessments can help you build teams where people process information differently. When used correctly, your awareness of this information will help you avoid what Adam Grant calls the inclination to hire for "cultural fit" and the "groupthink" team dynamic, both of which are counterproductive to innovation.[28]

On the other hand, understanding and engaging people with different backgrounds or human conditions provides you with insights on *behavioral* differences.[29] These differences are developed through our interactions with the environment. In other words, from experiences happening to individuals, based on who they are. For example: an extroverted (cognitive difference) Black/African American man in the US will most likely have a very different experience than an extroverted (again, cognitive difference) white man, if they are stopped by authorities while driving their car at 2:00 a.m.[30] Their racial human condition, and the consequences that similar actions have had in others who share that condition, will generate a *behavioral* impact on how they perceive not only the experience of driving at night, but of being stopped by the police.

This has always been a foundational debate in psychology theories. What defines who we are? Is it our genetic and physiological nature or our human experiences and conditioning? Choosing one over the other would be intellectually simplistic. From a practical perspective, it would also be quite limiting, if your intent is to use all relevant information to understand your employees, your clients and all other people around you.

My recommendation is not to justify a *diversity of thought* approach over *diversity of background and experiences*. Both schools of thought and practice can be part of your D&I strategy and leadership development efforts. As an additional consideration, keep in mind that the argument for primarily leaning toward *diversity of thought* can be interpreted as a subterfuge for an organization's weakness on other dimensions of diversity. By striving to create a demographic diversity of people's backgrounds and experiences, you can achieve **diversity of thought** *and* **diversity of thinkers**.

If you legitimately want to leverage human differences to spark innovation, stay true to your intent. If you want to generate the most positive impact for your organization, take an active approach in creating a safe, welcoming and inclusive environment where people can speak their minds and be listened to with respect.

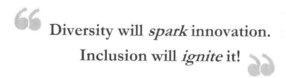

**Diversity will *spark* innovation.
Inclusion will *ignite* it!**

SEEKING THE POWER OF DIFFERENCES

For years, we've had research on the value of diverse thinking as a driver of company revenue and success. Below are some statistical data points that support this statement:

> "Research found that across hundreds of companies, diverse teams drive 6% greater revenue, 15% more customer wins, and create significantly higher market share. These teams work better together, innovate more, and come up with superior customer solutions."[31]

Forbes

> "When employees think their organization is committed to, and supportive of diversity and they feel included, employees report better business performance in terms of

ability to innovate (83% uplift), responsiveness to changing customer needs (31% uplift) and team collaboration (42% uplift)."[32]

Deloitte (Australia)

"Companies in the top quartile for gender or racial and ethnic diversity are more likely to have financial returns above their national industry medians."[33]

McKinsey

"In today's global business environment—filled with challenges in demographics, skills, and culture—companies that build a truly inclusive culture are those that will outperform their peers."[34]

Forbes

"Enabling employees to feel comfortable being themselves can unlock dramatic performance gains, because they can focus their attention on work, rather than hiding parts of themselves."[35]

Harvard Business Review

We have used this information and statistics to drive change, inform and influence leadership discussions, and activate plans to achieve greater diversity and inclusion in organizations.

When companies have the numbers to show progress in the diversity of their workforce and the inclusiveness of their culture, they should certainly be recognized and celebrated. This kind of change is *never* easy, so sharing accomplishments and best practices continues to be an important endeavor. Nonetheless, after leading D&I strategy and practice in several industries, I got used to hearing the same recommendations, the same solutions, the same practices, over and over again. At every conference, learning program, presentation, and panel discussion, the recommendations were the same. All-important premises to successfully lead D&I efforts were very similar in every company. The most common practices and recommendations are the same:

1. It's critical to have visible and active leadership support.
2. Develop clear metrics and tracking on the diversity of candidate slates, interview process, hiring, promotions, attrition/turnover.
3. Create a D&I Leadership Council.
4. Engage middle managers in action planning.
5. Ensure you create and support employee resource groups (ERGs).
6. Develop learning and development programs to drive awareness and change behaviors at all organizational levels.
7. Look for opportunities to drive business outcomes as well as employee engagement.
8. Make sure your company communications, internally and externally, reflect company values around diversity and inclusion.
9. Ensure to have visibility and engagement with external partners and suppliers that can support your D&I strategy.

10. Diversity is a journey, not a destination, that takes time and effort—so repeat the nine premises above!

These are all important and effective recommendations, but what else do we need? I certainly recognize we have to meet companies and leaders where they are, and in many cases, organizations are still scratching the surface in making progress around D&I efforts. They may have good intentions around D&I, but not as much focus on achieving the full impact of their efforts.

A recent study from Accenture revealed that when it comes to a workplace culture of inclusion, there is a large gap between what leaders think is going on and what employees say is happening on the ground:

> "Two thirds of leaders (68 percent) feel they create em-powering environments—in which employees can be themselves, raise concerns and innovate without fear of failure—but just one-third (36 percent) of employees agree."[36]

I've had the privilege of being part of organizations that had the intent, commitment, and talent to move the needle on their D&I goals. We led the efforts and built the metrics to prove it. However, I got the sense that there had to be more to it. For every success, there was also the risk and the disappointment of setbacks. So, if we were changing an organization's culture, we could also figure out ways to make those changes sustainable.

In the quest of discovery or creation of what's next in D&I, an increasing sense of impatience kept growing inside me. I wasn't waiting for some kind of revelation about it, but I couldn't stop thinking that something needed to be different. We could wait for the D&I journey to continue, for as long as it may take, or we could really think differently about differences (no pun intended), and how to create environments where *everyone* can contribute, where people feel valued not only for *what they know,* but also for *who they are;* not *in spite of* their differences, but *because* of their differences.

I'm not talking about a panacea. It's not utopia. I'm as practical as they come, but a few years ago, I got to the end of the impatience runway. I did not want to keep hearing that "we still have a lot of work to do" or "we have a long way to go." Well, let's get it done then! We shouldn't get complacent on a painfully slow and *transactional* evolution. We can think of a more *transformative* evolution of diversity and inclusion, where we experience the full positive impact of what research has proven we can accomplish. I kept asking myself the following questions:

From a business perspective:

- Why aren't we hearing the **specific stories,** not only from the researchers and consultants, but from the companies themselves, on how diversity and inclusion has actually **increased their revenue and financial results?**

- Why aren't we focusing more on understanding and replicating the mindsets and behaviors of the **positive deviants**[37]**who drive such results?**

- Why is it acceptable to say "we intend to" drive more inclusive work environments without insisting on **achieving the impact** we can derive from it?

From a leadership perspective:

- How can we disagree without disrespecting each other?

- How can we engage others (who are not like us) to get their ideas from the very beginning, instead of asking their perspective when our initial approach has failed?

- How can we genuinely learn how to build trust across our differences, and also make ourselves worthy of other people's trust?

- How can we change our business processes to create better solutions together, instead of (literally or mentally) point fingers at each other?

- How can we speak a new language to describe and create the inclusive environments we talk about so much?

Maybe you have asked yourself similar questions. So, what do you do?

For me, adding some perspiration to the inspiration of wanting to figure out what's next in D&I became a necessity, so I started taking notes.

For almost eight years now, I've been journaling leadership mindsets and behaviors, both constructive and destructive. But for the most part, I've analyzed behaviors that generate positive and sustainable impact in diversity and inclusion. I've looked at the behaviors of *formal* leaders, who have a job title that implies they will lead others, and *informal* leaders, who are natural, organic, and undeniable influencers of others, even without an official title for it. I explored and applied inclusive practices that transform the way we relate to each other, creating spaces where minds can truly generate better solutions for collective challenges.

This *can* be done, so why would you want to keep saying "we have a long way to go" if you can say "this is how we did it"? Leadership is not about complacency; it is about being better and bolder. Even if you don't feel you can change the world (at least not yet), you *can* create the best version of yourself and your work environment. Go ahead! Move from your best *intent* to your most unprecedented *impact*.

> 66 **Leadership is about *looking ahead* for what is possible, instead of *looking sideways* for what is around.** 99

CHAPTER 3
GETTING FROM INTENT TO IMPACT

One does not become enlightened by imagining
figures of light, but by making the darkness conscious.
The latter procedure, however, is disagreeable
and therefore, not popular.
—C. G. Jung

GOOD INTENTIONS ARE NOT ENOUGH

How many times have you heard that phrase, "It was not my intent"?

- "It was not my intent to imply that people in that community deserved the tragic event that just happened to them."

- "It was not my intent to offend people from that country when I made those comments."

- "In trying to be casual in my presentation, it was not my intent to use a joke that diminished the efforts of some of our teammates."

Too many times, leaders, celebrities and other public figures issue apologies that start that way and often go downhill from there. As part of my work with different organizations, I've provided guidance on **how to develop greater consciousness** about situations that required a public or private apology, on topics related to diversity and inclusion. In other words, to guide people on their thinking process, to create greater awareness and understanding of the negative impact of their words, their actions or inactions.

In their original form, the apologies I've reviewed sounded like the examples above. I'm sure you have heard this kind of "apology" many times, in conversations with family, friends, co-workers or even strangers. You most likely have used *"it was not my intent"* as well. Unfortunately, to the person or group of people to whom it is directed, it sounds as an excuse, not an apology. One of the reasons people perceive it that way it's because, as Stephen Covey reminds us, we don't listen with the **intent to *understand*,** but with **intent to *reply*,**[38] reinforce or defend our point of view. Even if you don't use these same words, apologies, either public or private, can go very wrong when your "intent to reply" looks like the following statements:

- "I understand you felt hurt by something I said/did. It was not my intent to hurt you. I didn't know you were sensitive about it."

- "I didn't mean to hurt you, so you must be hearing me wrong. I don't think I need to apologize. You just need to understand what I really meant."

- "I can't be responsible for the way everybody feels, and how my words impacted you. If you're sensitive about something I said, that's really on you, not on me."

These statements are generated from a mindset that strives to maintain some level of control in a situation that actually requires a different way of thinking, one guided by a **higher intent.** When you take time to review the situation based on its *impact*, you develop a more open mindset that goes beyond the appropriateness of an apology.

Lessons Learned

When seeking to understand why your words or actions had a negative impact or reaction on others, it is helpful to follow this approach:

- **Listen** to better understand the impact you have had on others.

- **Learn** to acknowledge your impact and open your mind to new information, even if it's painful, or embarrassing to do so.

- **Lead** by taking action to develop a "higher intent," focused on your desired impact.

Staying focused on that **higher intent,** one that goes beyond the justification of your actions, will guide your thoughts, your words and your approach towards a very different *impact*. This *higher intent* includes *active* and *reflective* listening,[39] where you mirror/ acknowledge the impact a situation had on a person, suspend judgment about how they feel about it and create new space for deeper and more effective communication. For example, you might then say:

- "I understand you felt hurt by something I said/did. I never meant for this to happen, but I recognize the impact it had on you, and I'm very sorry about it. What can I do to mitigate the impact?"

- "I didn't mean to offend you, but realize my words/actions had a negative impact on you. After reflecting on it, I learned something I think can help me do differently in the future. May I share that learning with you and get your feedback?"

- "I take responsibility for the negative impact that my words/actions had on you. Please accept my apologies. What can I do differently to prevent this from happening again?

This approach will help you drive toward a more positive impact in situations when you honestly didn't necessarily know or anticipate the reactions of others. But what about situations when *others* don't necessarily know enough about *you*? How do you go about developing your *own* positive impact in moving forward, without holding resentment or frustration about how others may have made *you* feel? Let's look into it.

WHAT ACCENT?

At the very beginning of this book, I shared a few lines about how the "accent advice" took me by surprise. My accent had not been an issue up to that point. After that piece of advice, I was put on notice it would, however, be something I would have to think about moving forward. While a part of me felt angry about it, I also remember asking myself: *Am I ungrateful for the sincerity of the advice that I asked for? Am I being too sensitive? Do I need to "toughen up" to climb the corporate ladder?* It's not easy to figure out the ambivalence of anger and self-doubt.

Even when the advice may have been given with positive intent, it also revealed signs of a work environment that was not as inclusive as it could have been. Situations like this one have improved in many organizations, but not in others. We have more leaders who understand the value of such differences, but many others still don't. Even worse, they may not even be conscious about it.

As a professional, if this would have happened to you, what would you do? Or if you were in the position of the leader I asked for advice, how would you handle it?

Aside from my own personal story, take what scientists have learned about how our brains process foreign accents, and then, add negative stereotypes into the mix. One of the most pervasive tendencies all of us have is to equate intelligence, skills, and leadership abilities with language fluency. If a person's fluency is limited, many of us incorrectly assume their other capacities are limited as well. Yet, a study conducted by University of Chicago psychologists on how language affects reasoning reveals that people who think in a second language make decisions that actually tend to be less biased, more analytic, and more systematic. Why is that? Because, according to the study's lead author Boaz Keysar, "thinking in a foreign language provides *psychological distance*. Cognitive biases are rooted in emotional reactions, and thinking in a foreign language helps us disconnect from these emotions and make decisions in a more economically rational way," he explained.[40]

The common assumption of many native speakers is that people who struggle with a second (third or fourth) language, also struggle with intelligence. For starters, when we are not used to an accent, it's a bit harder for our brain to process what the speaker is saying. Secondly, we tend to have a negative bias against some accents.

Shiri Lev-Ari, a psycholinguist at the Max Planck Institute of Psycholinguistics in Nijmegen, found that native English speakers rated speakers with the heaviest accents as least truthful. She has also conducted research showing that native speakers remember less accurately what non-native speakers say. So, yes, it may be a bit hard to overcome the impact one's accent has on someone else's brain. Nonetheless, Lev-Ari also points out that the more we're exposed to foreign accents, the more our brains train themselves to process the speech more efficiently. In as little as four minutes, a person can improve how much they understand of speech with a foreign accent.

So, while our brains can adapt quite quickly to different accents, people's stereotypes take a lot longer to change.[41] Simply put, not all accents are perceived as equal. In the US, a British accent is regarded very differently than a Southern US accent. One is perceived as inherently "smart" and even "sexy."[42] The other may be perceived as "charming," but "less educated."[43]

We must then recognize there are two distinctive issues with accents:

- A psycholinguistic **understanding** of the content being communicated with a foreign accent.

- The **value and validity** adjudicated to the content communicated with that foreign accent.

Ultimately then, when someone has been frequently exposed to a foreign accent, a prevalent negative or hyper-positive reaction to it can be a sign of a deeper stereotype or bias against or towards those who have that accent. Research shows different languages focus the attention of their speakers on different aspects of their environment—either physical or cultural.[44] Being conscious about this reality can help you learn more about yourself, and be a leader who more effectively values and leverages diversity.

Lessons Learned

Check yourself! Do your own personal experiment. Next time you have:

- A **negative reaction** to someone's accent: Does it bother you? Does it distract you? Does it make you angry?

- A **hyper positive reaction** to someone's accent: Does it make you smile? Do you find it charming? Do you feel compelled to mimic it?

You have an opportunity to create greater consciousness about it, explore what stereotypes may be influencing your reactions, and build a more balanced and informed experience for yourself and others in moving forward.

Since I didn't want to have a permanent chip on my shoulder about *my* accent, I asked myself the same question I'm asking you: how do you go about developing your *own* positive impact, without holding resentment or frustration about how others may have made *you* feel? Like many other people, I believe things happen for a reason, and a future job opportunity gave me the chance to create a different "accent experience" and *impact* for others.

WHAT ENGLISH?

A few years later, I had transitioned to a new company and a different industry. Part of my responsibility in this role was to oversee the curriculum of diversity and inclusion learning programs. As such, I was meeting with external vendors who facilitated learning offerings that were part of our existing strategy. I remember a particular day, as I was coming back to my office for a mid-morning meeting with one of these vendors, we had a conversation I will never forget.

This vendor was offering us a "diversity and inclusion program" that was quite popular. It focused on supporting international hires in their onboarding process. I was looking forward to knowing more about this program, to understand why it was such a coveted offering.

I completely (and personally) understood the strong desire international new hires have to "blend in" as quickly as they can. For many of them, the process of being hired in the US was long. First, they would have to get noticed by the company they hoped would hire them. This would be followed by several trips to complete a lengthy interview process. And then, there is the negotiation of a job offer, work visas, relocation (that many times required uprooting a whole family), and more. Needless to say, in these situations, the financial as well as personal stakes are high.

Achieving early indicators that the whole hiring and relocation endeavor held strong potential for success is important to both the employee and the company. In this particular case, I was glad to know we were paying special attention to the needs of international hires, so my disposition coming into the meeting was positive. However, the only thing I was a bit puzzled about was the program's title: "Learning American English."

After the usual introductions and professional rapport-building exchange, the vendor shared a general outline of the program. It became clear, after reviewing the details, that the intent to accelerate employees' onboarding was there, but a few elements of the instructional design conflicted a bit. For example, as we began our conversation, the vendor proudly stated: "On this program, we help people speak American English, particularly when English is not their first language."

Through the vendor's explanation, I realized her goal was to help people change the intonation or enunciation they give to different words, so they could more easily be understood by people around them who are born in the US or only speak English. The *intent* behind the program was good. Out of legitimate curiosity, though, I then asked: "Which American English should I understand you're referencing? Is that English spoken by people in our nearest city? The one we hear in the southern part of the country? Or is it more like East Coast English?" This led to the question, "What exactly is American English?'"

Again, the value that training like this brings to people who want to enhance their verbal communication can be quite high. I understood the premise, but there was something here that was not landing well for me—the way we were going about that positive intent.

As the vendor further explained the program, she said: "People have come here because they are very technically capable. In order to progress in their careers, however, they have to adapt the way they speak." This meant we were, literally, telling people who we hired from different parts of the world because of their talent, skills, and abilities that in order to succeed in the company, they needed to change a very basic human skill—the way they speak.

What disturbed me most was the way this concept was presented during the program. The approach essentially validated an underlying message of "even though you may be very talented, we need you to unlearn and relearn some foundational things that you learned as a toddler." It seemed that some people had no issue with this, or if they did, they kept it to themselves. They were willing to change who they were, how they spoke, maybe even how they presented themselves, in order to fit in, to be accepted, to succeed. I remembered my own first glint of awareness and then struggle to decide how much I was willing to give up to adapt or change to fit in.

Although I'm an advocate for self-discovery and human reinvention, there was still something that felt wrong about this approach. Why would we have to tell people they had to sound more like others, instead of becoming an enhanced version of themselves? Why did we need to ask people to become more homogeneous in the way they spoke, when we could instead help them build on their ability to speak two, three, four or more languages?

Pressing to find a different way of addressing the needs of our linguistically diverse talent, I asked the vendor, "How many languages do you speak? Additionally, the people who are training others on how to do this, how many languages do they speak?" She responded, "Well, we speak English."

I realized it was somewhat difficult for the vendor to fully understand my concerns about this (even though I tried to explain it, in more than one way). This was not their personal experience, so they couldn't relate to it. It appeared as though they hadn't considered the impact on their program recipients. Unintentional actions can have a strong impact on people. This was one of those times. Even though I didn't want to generalize my "you should work on your accent" experience for everyone who speaks multiple languages, I was the only one there at the time to make this point. I was also certain I would not be the only person who would think that way.

As some business colleagues know, "accent reduction" offerings have not been uncommon. In certain roles, particularly customer-facing jobs, you can find books, recordings and a variety of coaches who offer help to those who would like to "lose their accent." It's not just for foreign-language speakers, but also regional fluctuations within the same language. For example, in the US, if you're from the South and listen to someone from Maine, or Wisconsin, you may find that their accents are (initially) as difficult to understand as someone from France or Germany speaking English. Interestingly enough, France and the United Kingdom have also had public discourse and research to address accent bias, accent discrimination, and its impact on access to elite professions.[45] The most important element to keep in mind is that, while a different pronunciation or accent within your native language is easier to change, most researchers agree that, as an adult, acquiring a native-like accent of a second language is nearly impossible.[46]

Even though our company and our vendor had good intentions in offering the "American English" program, the path we were traveling down could have an unintended negative impact. The way the program was designed could communicate conflicting messages. We needed to use a different approach, to convey that we valued every talent people brought to the organization. We had to find a way to ensure our learning offerings would *empower* people, not diminish their self-esteem and confidence in their ability to succeed in our company.

> ❝ **Confidence is a vulnerable state of mind:**
> **it takes time and effort to build,**
> **but it can be diminished by subtle micro-messages**
> **coming your way.** ❞

Starting from an appreciation mindset, I walked through the following thought process:

- **Essential facts.** We had a large group of employees who could communicate in more than one language. Two of the reasons we hired them were their cultural dexterity and multi-language skills. These were necessary to better understand and connect with our customers, provide them a more personalized experience and build a preference and loyalty for our company.

- **Value mindset.** If we thought about language as part of our human capital, this would mean our multilingual employees would have the "fluency to increase our currency." Their multilingual capabilities represented an abundance of language capital for our company. What they brought to the table was an asset, not a deficiency.

- **Impact delivery.** We had the opportunity to ensure a more positive impact. With that value-mindset, we could develop a better way to communicate our *intent* towards these employees: Provide them guidance on how to manage their multilingual abilities as assets. This would in turn pay dividends in their career progression and our company's success.

Combining facts with a value mindset, we would have a program that accomplished a better version of our *intent,* and have a more positive impact on our skill development, building confidence and self-esteem at the same time. Coming up with an appropriate name for the program was then quite easy: "Learning American English" was replaced by "Managing Your Language Capital."

THE REAL VALUE OF INTENT

As I mentioned before, good intentions are not enough. While impact is the ultimate goal when we seek to understand human differences, it is also important to adequately position the *value* of your *intent* — the *higher intent* that I mentioned earlier in this chapter.

For example, if you have been diagnosed with hypertension, you may tell your physician you *intend* to exercise more or change your diet. You may not do much to immediately act on it, but without an intentional decision to do so, you will be left with a permanent concern about your systolic and diastolic numbers. There is real value in your intent. It's a necessary first step to achieve your goals.

That is the reason leaders tend to share their vision early in the process of engaging with those they lead. It describes what you intend to achieve, and what you will ask others to do to help reach those goals. In absence of this information, people "fill the void" of information with speculation and doubt, which hinders your ability to create trust within a team. Even more, without a clear statement of intent (vision or goals), people may experience the negative impact of suspicion, anxiety and concern. They will question if your intent includes caring for them as much as they expect you will care for the business.

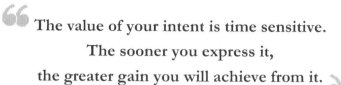

**The value of your intent is time sensitive.
The sooner you express it,
the greater gain you will achieve from it.**

In this sense, diversity and inclusion are no different than any other vision or goal in the organization. It must be intentional. It requires a **leadership declaration** of your *intent* that answers key questions employees may have about you, such as the following:

- Why do you **care** about building a diverse workforce or an inclusive work environment? Why is it **important** to you as a leader? Why is it important to the organization?

- What are your **expectations** on key D&I outcomes to be achieved in the short or long term? What **actions** will you take or ask us to take to make them happen?

- What is the **competence** level of the organization to drive greater diversity and inclusion? What do you expect people to **learn, unlearn, change,** or **create** to achieve greater diversity and inclusion?

As Anese Cavanaugh reminds us in her book *Contagious Culture,* when speaking about intentional leadership: "The more connected you are to yourself, and the clearer you are on what kind of impact you want to have, the easier it is to hold your space and lead intentionally."[47] Of this statement, I find most relevance on the element of being "connected to yourself." That is why leaders who intend to leverage diversity and inclusion as a business driver must be, at least, consciously competent about themselves.

CONSCIOUSNESS AND COMPETENCE

In the learning field, the **four stages of competence** refer to the psychological states involved in the process of progressing from incompetence to competence in a particular skill:[48]

- **Stage 1: Unconscious Incompetence**—I don't know what I don't know

- **Stage 2: Conscious Incompetence**—I know what I don't know

- **Stage 3: Conscious Competence**—I know, I'm growing and it's showing

- **Stage 4: Unconscious Competence**—What I know is now second nature to me

You would expect formal leaders in organizations to be competent in the most crucial skills to do their jobs. This includes being fully aware of how they come across to others—how their words, their actions, and even their inactions affect those whom they have the privilege to lead. That is the reason we have executive coaches, career coaches, life coaches, 360-degree assessments, emotional intelligence evaluations, implicit association tests (IAT) and other behavioral and cognitive evaluations.[49]

Most people could live their whole lives without necessarily being deep learners about themselves. Effective leaders, on the other hand, can't afford the same "luxury" (no pun intended). Leading with intent should *start* with the deepest understanding of themselves—because these "selves" have a considerable impact in the lives of many others.

It may sound a bit harsh to say that someone, particularly a leader, is unconscious or incompetent on any particular topic. Putting labels on each other is not the purpose of this book. At this point, our focus is to guide those whose *intent* is to reap the benefits of diversity and inclusion, to have the greatest impact in their organizations and their lives. As I said before, let's direct our attention to being knowledgeable about *ourselves,* before we talk about being knowledgeable about *others.* In other words, this starts with ensuring we have greater understanding of the dimensions of human differences that are most **relevant to us** at any given point. This may sound too theoretical, so let me share a few real-life examples.

FROM MICHELANGELO TO GOLDFISH

UNCONSCIOUS INCOMPETENCE

A relatively young leader (I believe he was in his mid-30s) in technology was not making much headway in working with his team. He was deemed to be a "difficult person to work with." As a result, my Human Resources colleague and I approached him to discuss ways he could foster better team engagement. Our recommendations included encouraging him to complete a 360-degree evaluation and to discuss elements of emotional intelligence. Although we knew about his "personality," we still expected him to ask, "What should I do differently?" In other words, we were driving toward greater openness to exploring options he had not previously considered.

As we opened the conversation, a key statement we made was: "Leaning into this learning approach could go a long way towards improving team collaboration and results." To my surprise, his response was, "Well, I'm really focusing on what it is that I could *ask them* to do differently, or that *they should* do differently. I don't feel I need to change, as I think of myself as already being my best finished product."

I almost did a double take as I looked at him incredulously and pondered, *Okay, I don't think I heard right. How could someone say, 'I'm already my best finished product?'* I whispered to my HR colleague, "He's kidding, right?" I could tell that she was as flabbergasted as I was. Needless to say, his "Michelangelo arrogance" didn't seem to be accompanied by the sculptor's paradoxical dissatisfaction with himself.[50] Even though he was already at an executive level, this leader was still a relatively young person, not uncommon in the high-tech field.

How could someone living and breathing the continuous evolution of technology and innovation fail to see the need to apply that same principle of innovation, iteration, and learning to himself? The sheer hubris of it was staggering. Our conclusion? He just *didn't know what he didn't know* about himself.

Many of us have been part of the broad trend of corporate discussion and learning offerings about unconscious (implicit) bias. It's been a part of the diversity and inclusion repertoire for years now. A few premises about unconscious bias are:[51]

- Everyone possesses bias.

- Most people are unaware of it.

- It is deeply ingrained.

- It influences attitudes and behaviors.

- It can be quantified.

In other words, unconscious bias is an example of unconscious incompetence. Even though it is still something we all possess, when we refer to leaders, it is critically important to address individual and organizational biases, to have a positive impact in selecting, managing and leading teams as well and leading business.

While few people may be as cavalier in their statements as my "techy Michelangelo," this thought pattern exists amongst many. Without an *intent* to learn and be invested in a *personal* evolution, we cannot reach our greatest *impact*. For leaders who truly aspire to achieve their highest level of impact, it is critically important to continuously learn about themselves and about others.

CONSCIOUS INCOMPETENCE

A few years ago, I was designing a customized development program for an operations leadership team of around ten people. They were all seasoned executives. A couple of them had been part of the team for over a decade, and could almost complete each other's sentences. Others had recently joined the department and a few of them were recent external hires.

Those who were new to the department were still trying to identify the way this team operated, and those who were new to the company were eager to score with their first quick wins. As they approached me for support, they were clear on their intent. They were at the forefront of a crucial cost-savings initiative for the company. They needed to ensure they were leveraging the full spectrum of talents and perspectives each of them brought to the team.

I designed an exercise to help them gain a deeper understanding of characteristics that represented uniqueness and/ or commonalities with their other team members. Part of the goal was to find elements that were not currently being leveraged within their team. It was intended to be an exercise of discovery, and discovery was what we got.

While still in the planning phase, I selected a visual aid to use during the program. It was the image of a goldfish, swimming in a clear fishbowl, surrounded by several blue fish. The statement this image would prompt was simple: "Tell me about a time when you felt different."

As I was explaining the program outline to the most senior leader of the group, he saw the image of the goldfish, and somberly asked: "Why did you pick a photo of me?" It was clear he wasn't trying to be funny. I respectfully asked, "I'm not sure I understand… What do you mean 'a picture of you'?" He replied, "That's me. That goldfish right there." His facial expression quickly transformed. He went to a deep place in his mind, as he explained, "That is me when

I was a child. I was a redhead, a ginger, and I was bullied for that. I was bullied for a long time."

After a solemn pause, his response opened up a whole new conversation. It would have been difficult to anticipate his reaction and even more, his answer. What may have been a clear pheomelanin hair pigment in his youth was now a silvery crew-cut that perfectly paired his military leadership style. Two of his direct reports, who were with me that day, spearheading this leadership program, learned something quite important they never knew about their leader. Not just the fact that he was a bullied redhead, but how deeply he *still* felt about it.

It was clear that he was keenly aware, deeply conscious about that experience of being bullied because of the color of his hair. Nonetheless, in previous conversations he had firmly stated how ignorant he felt about the experience of African Americans in the company. Not having the experience of being treated differently because of the color of his skin, he didn't consider the opportunity to engage in that topic—not even as a learning opportunity! While he could have used his own experience as a starting point to understand the feeling of being different, he didn't. He knew what he knew, but had the humility to admit what he didn't know.

From that point, we evolved to a more refined version of the *intent* we had for the program. It went beyond "leveraging the full spectrum of talents and perspectives each of them brought to the team." What we had learned from this leader revealed a vulnerability that immediately made him more personable, more real and approachable in the eyes of the team members who were part of the conversation that day. The *impact* we would have from learning about each other was now a lot deeper, a lot more personal, and that was a more positive outcome for this team.

FROM HUDDLERS TO WISDOM SEEKERS

CONSCIOUS COMPETENCE

Even before I started working in sports media, I was curious about organizations where you could experience a "team culture" versus an "most valuable player (MVP) culture." Distinguishing between the two actually became a very important factor to determine my interest in job opportunities within an organization. When interviewing for a job, I would ask for examples of their culture: words they used to describe their interactions, habits they followed to get work done, principles or values that guided their behaviors. I would check how many times people made reference to their MVPs (or "rock stars"), people who are "killing it," or people who are "winners." This sat in contrast with cultures that made more reference to *networks, task forces, cohorts,* and *huddles.*

In sports, particularly American or Canadian football as well as cricket, a huddle is formed when a team gathers together to discuss a game plan, motivate each other or celebrate a victory. The huddle is a tight space, a cluster, where information is shared in a "circle of trust" that keeps opponents away from sensitive information, particularly in a noisy on-field environment. It's a visible sign of a team culture. It happens often, it is expected, it has a clear intent and impact.

For a long time, the world of sports and entertainment has been the scenario where many of the dilemmas of diversity and inclusion have taken center stage. We follow the lives and accomplishments of our favorite athletes. We take pride in their success. They become role models of courage, discipline and perseverance, for our children and ourselves.

In the US, sports have also become a platform for social advocacy, where athletes raise their voices against inequalities, in and out of the field. Athletes like Venus Williams,[52] Michael Sam,[53] Colin Kaepernick,[54] and the US Women's Soccer Team[55] have become known not only for their performance on their respective sports, but also for their advocacy on resetting standards that perpetuate social and economic inequalities. Their performance and activism have created conflict, and established precedents at the same time.

The era of #MeToo and #BlackLivesMatter, pay equality, and gender transitions implies that diversity and inclusion is constantly in the public eye. Leading diversity and inclusion in the sports media industry gave me the opportunity to act on the undeniable necessity to be a clear voice in the discussion of these topics. We didn't have the luxury of being anything less than competent when reporting on these stories. These were some of the everyday questions we had to think about:

- Is it appropriate to reference the use of the "N word" in our reporting?

- What is more important in covering stories of Latino athletes? That the reporter is Latino/a or that he/she is able to speak Spanish?

- Should we keep the camera on the team when they are praying on the field before the game?

- Do we show the kiss between the LGBTQ athlete and his partner?

- What would be the best approach when reporting on allegations of domestic violence that involve top athletes?

- How do we reach a balance between reporting on stories and becoming part of the story?

- How do we balance journalistic intent and entertaining impact when dealing with topics of human interest, of diversity and inclusion?

So how do you do that? How do you build an environment where there is continuous learning on topics of human interest and impact that are rapidly changing as well? There was no other option than to be (at least) *consciously competent* on any topic related to diversity and inclusion. We had to strategize, discuss the plan before every season and every game. We needed to ensure each team member knew how to do their best in their position, and be ready to complement each other, so we could score and win. In other words, we *huddled*.

Our D&I huddles started as a team development program. The Huddles were convened by leaders who were extremely intentional in the acceleration of their knowledge about human differences that were part of the stories they were covering; of the content they were creating. The D&I huddles provided a space where people would be able to engage with candor, speak truth to power and challenge each other with care, practicing inclusive leadership behaviors that would ensure they could get the best of what everyone had to offer in the team.

This was actual practice and application, not merely awareness building. It was designed for teams that were *consciously competent* visionaries and innovators; they knew what they knew and wanted to lead in this space, by accelerating their learning. They were the huddlers, the ones who were on it and who would lead the pace for others.

Lessons Learned

- **Engage and practice:** Create internal forums for inclusive conversations. Aside from the D&I huddles, you can find valuable examples in the *Intergroup Dialogue* programs at Cornell University[56] and Syracuse University.[57]

- **Respect and value, before challenge:** Show respect and value for your teammates before challenging their thinking. This will help you keep their engagement.

UNCONSCIOUS COMPETENCE

You recognize mastery when you see it. You notice when people use their skills and talents in ways that seem effortless, unconsciously competent, as if their flawless performance was second nature to them. We attribute it to people who are thought leaders, innovators, or exceptional performers who are highly successful in their fields, but you can sometimes find mastery in everyday interactions.

I remember a dinner in Harlem, New York, with a group of business colleagues. It was not a company function or sponsored event, so our respective partners were also invited. My husband and I were anticipating it would become a unique experience: the chef, the menu, and the open environment were all promising elements of that summer afternoon.

We quickly engaged in an open and casual conversation that got increasingly louder. At one point, the blend of music, outside traffic, and noise of metal utensils cutting over porcelain plates made it difficult to hear each other. In the middle of multiple conversations happening at the same time, something caught my attention: the spouse of one of my colleagues asked me, "Can you tell me more about that?" Honestly, I didn't even remember what I'd said. At first, I felt flattered that she was so attentive to my words, even in the middle of all that noise. Then, I observed the unique and consistent way she handled the conversations she had with others as well. You could see how she was fully engaged in every exchange she had.

Having been in countless dinners and networking events, this struck me as something very different. Instead of being distracted by noise, she was fully present and visibly focused on the person she was speaking with, ensuring you knew she was interested in what you had to say. I took notice of how she used a slower pace and slightly lower volume to move with ease under the cloud of noisy and rapid exchange around us. She would connect and react to what you said, and how you said it. When others interjected, she would flawlessly make a slight redirection of the conversation, to ensure every voice was heard. This was noticeably different from the norm. I was in the presence of mastery in inclusion.

How people achieve a level of mastery in any field has been highly debated.[58] Authors like Malcolm Gladwell,[59] Frans Johannsson[60] and Daniel Goleman[61] have attributed mastery to an insane amount of practice, sparks of originality that seem random, or great self-awareness and self-control. These theories don't necessarily contradict each other. They complement each other. The complexity of human behaviors and capabilities cannot be explained with a single approach. What we also know about many successful people who are perceived as masters in their fields is that they are incredibly curious.[62] They are constant learners.[63] They practice what you could call "**wisdom seeking**."

I'm sure you know who those *wisdom seekers* are. They are people who are never satisfied with what they already know. They look for new learnings in areas they already master or insert themselves in new areas of knowledge, to feel the thrill of being novices again.

Some will go beyond their own mastery, step out of the norms, break the rules and, intentionally or not, revolutionize their fields.

If you see yourself as a **huddler** or **wisdom seeker,** you are already committed to constant curiosity about human differences. You will intentionally focus your learning in understanding how to generate the greatest impact on others, with others, through others, in anything you do. That is what distinguishes those who lead from those who follow. Huddlers and wisdom seekers, who are already consciously or unconsciously competent in leading teams and leading businesses, might be the first ones to pick this book, as you did.

Lessons Learned

Ask yourself:

- Are you a *huddler* or a *wisdom seeker?*
- Are you trying to *keep the pace* of your diversity and inclusion efforts or are you *seeking the next frontier* of what the power of human differences can achieve?
- Are you clear on your *intent?*
- Do you have a *higher intent?*
- Are you ready for your *impact?*

PART TWO

THE 5 DUALITIES OF
DIVERSITY AND INCLUSION

Idris: Are all people like this?
The Doctor: Like what?
Idris: So much bigger on the inside.
—Neil Gaiman, *Dr. Who*

5 DUALITIES TO DRIVE YOUR D&I IMPACT

As we move from a better understanding of your *intent* to creating your most positive *impact* on others, I will describe and give you examples for each of the five dualities of diversity and inclusion. As you learn about the dualities, remember the following premises:

- A duality is about having two parts, which is where the "dual" comes from.

- The elements of each D&I duality are not in opposition. They actually complement each other.

- Each D&I duality represents the fluctuation and/ or evolution of your mindset.

As I mentioned in the introduction of this book, the five dualities of diversity and inclusion are complementary to each other, as five parts of your brain.

D&I Duality	Is similar to:	That focuses on:	To achieve the following:
1. Connect & Learn	Cerebellum	Balance	Balance between your similarities and your differences from other people.
2. Think & Know	Frontal lobe	Judgment	Judge between your observations and your conclusions about people.
3. Pain & Possibility	Parietal lobe	Sensation	Minimize the sensation of pain, but also consider the possibilities of positive impact on your work environment.
4. Risk & Invest	Occipital lobe	Vision	View diversity and inclusion as a way to manage potential risks, but also a way to invest in your talent portfolio.
5. Perform & Innovate	Temporal lobe	Hearing and Behaviors	Move from hearing about diversity as "noise" that slows down your performance, to leading with inclusive behaviors that truly ignite innovation.

CHAPTER 4

DUALITY 1: CONNECT AND LEARN

"Hi, it's nice to meet you..."

"What company are you in?"

"What is your role there?"

"How long have you been at your organization?"

"How long have you lived in this area?"

Think about your most recent business networking experience. Did it sound anything like this? How about the most recent meeting where someone new was joining the conversation? Did it sound similar to this series of foundational questions?

Asking for this kind of information is a necessary habit when getting to know someone in a business setting. We've all asked these questions and responded to them as well. Even when you and I recognize the importance and value of meeting new people, we still dread the monotonous five-to eight-word questions of every introduction, which is the way most networking sessions go.

Introductory questions provide basic information on the other person, which makes perfect sense for networking. What is most interesting, and sometimes quite amusing, is to observe how an introductory conversation actually unfolds:

"Hi, it's nice to meet you. What is your role in your company?"

"I work in Sales & Marketing."

"Nice! I started my career in Sales as well. How long have you been at your company?"

"I've been there for only a year. Before this, I used to work at a pharmaceutical company."

"Really? Me too, which company?"

"XYZ Pharma."

"Oh! I know someone there. Jeremy Lang, from Procurement. Do you know him?"

"Yes, I know Jeremy. We worked together on a project for the past six months."

And so on…

For years, I have been conducting my very own social experiment, listening and exploring patterns of communication that create human connection, both at a professional and personal level. The person responding to these introductory questions can either be brief or verbose, provide two- or three-word answers, or tell a whole story in every answer. The person who initially asks the questions may listen attentively to the information being provided, but most of the time, answers will be interrupted the very minute the listener hears a familiar term: a name, a concept, a location—anything that triggers a connection to something important or familiar to them.

At that precise moment, the flow of information probably shifts, and the person originally asking the questions now provides the answers, as they apply on a personal level. From there, the exchange may bifurcate in many ways, depending on the personality and sensitivity of those in the conversation. You will undoubtedly see that the more points of connection two people find in the conversation, the longer they'll keep talking. The more emotionally engaged they will seem to be in the conversation. That is how relationships are built.

Even with people who tend to be more private or cautions in sharing personal information, the exchange typically follows a similar path: in business settings, when we meet a new neighbor, go to a friend's gathering, and so on. Once you find a similarity between yourself and someone else, you will often start going down a path of connections, areas of interest or common purpose you may have with that person. If the conversation reveals you don't have a common interest in a sport, a team, a hobby or TV series, you will most likely take the conversation in a different direction, in an attempt to keep the connecting energy flowing. It is the natural (sometimes called organic) way people meet and talk to each other, with the intent to efficiently sift through information of potential value, to you or the person you're speaking to, and that's all okay.

At first, I didn't really pay too much attention to the predictability of this kind of transactional exchange. I just took it for granted, as you probably do as well. But after years of engaging in professional networking sessions and business meetings, I started to pay more attention to two elements: the valuable information that is left out of those short exchanges between two individuals and the amount of people that typically get sidelined from these conversations when they happen in a group setting.

How many times have you been at a business dinner where people spend most of their time talking only with the person sitting right next to them, working on those initial "transactional connections" I just mentioned? I guess that's why those tables are set for an even number of seats—so each person can "pick a pair" to speak with. When you're at a networking session, which are typically standing events, you may find triads of people attempting a similar exchange. More times than not, two people will be building a transactional connection and the third one will be trying to figure out how to engage in the conversation in a more active way. But building connections doesn't have to be that predictable. It is a practice that can actually create deeper learning about something or someone, but we are less wired to insert ourselves deeply into something that is less known, because it can be quite uncomfortable to do so.

CONNECTING THROUGH OUR SIMILARITIES

I remember the conversation with Jack. I was attending a three-day leadership program at the company. At the end of the first day, we had one of those ten-people-per-table business dinners I just referenced. Looking around the table where I was seated, I realized there were only two women seated there and I was one of them. Right next to me, was one of the most senior leaders of the organization. He had been at the company for decades. He knew everybody and everybody knew him, but since I had just joined the company, this was the first time I would have a conversation with him, after our initial introduction.

As the typical "transactional conversation" started, the first topic was football. I don't necessarily consider myself a sports fan. I'm more of a sports enthusiast, but I had just joined the worldwide leader in sports (yes, I will mention the name this time). It was ESPN. I was just getting to know this leader, so where could I start a conversation?

If this had happened a few months later, when I had already immersed myself in knowing as much as I could about the National Football League (NFL), it would have been much easier, but that was not the case. Of course, I wanted to make a good impression, to sound smart and be memorable (in a good way). With a flow of ideas running through my head, I realized: *Okay, he knows about all these teams, but I don't know (yet) which ones he likes best. No... I'm not going to look at the other woman at this table hoping we can connect on another topic. She knows sports as well as they do!* I knew I could comment on a few teams and maybe some of the most prominent players, but in the company of people who live and breathe the sports culture, I felt like a rookie sitting on the sidelines. I had not yet accumulated enough knowledge (maybe I never will) to sound like a "sports native," but here I was, in a different culture, mingling with the experts.

After a few minutes and a deep breath, I finally landed on a useful thought: I can't (or won't) start a conversation on a topic that is not familiar to me. I cannot "be one of them" right now. Not on that topic, but I can find a different connection. I don't need to feel intimidated! I'm here for a very good reason. So, I started a conversation in a more natural way. Since I had just relocated to take the job, I broke the ice by asking, "Hey Jack. Are you originally from Connecticut?" A whole new conversation started, one where I felt safe and comfortable.

We are all inclined to connect with people on areas where we can find common ground - experiences, values, background, preferences and even traits of our personality. That is how we select friends, engage in love relationships, identify social groups we want to be a part of, make decisions about companies to work for and teams we want to join. Either consciously or unconsciously, connecting on our similarities creates psychological safety. The more similarities you see, the greater psychological safety you will perceive. You build connections based on what you have in common with the other person, before you explore differences that may be a bit difficult to talk about. Once you've built rapport with the other person, it is easier (and even more appropriate) to explore your differences.[64] This is how our brains are wired, to mitigate the perceived risks of dealing with the unknown.[65]

The challenge is that, when differences are immediately visible (such as a physical disability, attire that reflects culture or beliefs, or facial features we associate with a race or ethnicity), you will most likely *see* the differences *before* you look for similarities. You will see the disability, before you see the person with the disability. We see the hijab, before you see the woman wearing it. In a nanosecond, we make conscious or unconscious decisions about who to speak with *first* in that meeting, in that conference room or networking session. The result of this dynamic is a diminished opportunity for those who have visible differences to build connections, when they may be the only ones or the very few in a group that does not look like them. In a space where the whole purpose is to make connections or engage in valuable exchange, people who are visibly different from the majority in that group will most likely have to double the attempts to connect with others, to compensate for the attempts that others may *not* make to connect with them. This is hardly a level playing field.

This is the dilemma that led me to articulate the **Duality 1: Connect and Learn.** Think about it as the foundation of the five dualities. Remember what I said earlier: Connect and Learn is the base where the other four dualities sit. It's like the *cerebellum*. On D&I, your goal must be to seek a balance between our similarities and our differences.

In the organizational practice of diversity and inclusion, it is common to support the natural need for people to connect through their similarities. That is one of the reasons companies and organizations have continued to sponsor employee resource groups (ERG),[66] development conferences targeted for women, LGBTQ, people with disabilities, and so on. In the US, this also includes the practice of having leadership development programs and forums for racial/ethnic minority groups. These practices respond to a historic reality of workplaces where people in these groups have traditionally not had a sense of connection or belonging. Work environments where they don't typically see "people like me"—people who think, look, feel, behave, talk, dress "like me"—in the corporate world. It's this feeling of belonging, of fitting in, what individuals typically seek and find in these groups.

While the existence of these "groups of connection" has been challenged in recent times,[67] I would argue that the attempt to eliminate them from the corporate environment, with the proclaimed good *intent* to advance inclusion, is an exercise of retrocession. The actual *impact* of this practice carries the unintended consequence of lowering the volume of voices that for so long have tried to be heard, to understand and become part of corporate cultures that were built with a mindset that is very different from theirs. I don't see the solution as *having* or *not having* these groups and forums of connection. It is a matter of having them *and* also building mechanisms to break barriers created by our differences, not by the need for connection that drove the creation of these groups in the first place.

Our similarities are the undeniable way in which we more easily connect with other people.[68] However, if not managed properly, our similarities to others can also become a limitation, an impediment to further expand our thinking, to build new layers of learning about others.

From an intellectual and behavioral perspective, when you excessively rely on the notion that what you think is shared by others (who happen to be like you), you run the risk of *believing* that your perceptions are the "right ones" or the "best ones" for everyone. You can get the false impression that "if I'm right" and "know many people who think like me," those who think or behave differently must "be wrong." This behavior contributes to the great polarization of thoughts and actions we see in people, even between those who otherwise like or love each other. Your opportunity is to not overwhelmingly rely on your thinking or emotional connections to others, based on your similarities with them. Doing so would underestimate the greater human capability you have to learn from people who are different from you.

While we find comfort in our similarities, our opportunity to further expand our learning about others is through our differences. But in most instances, the opportunity to learn from our differences requires a *higher intent,* a legitimate interest to understand and relate with those around us. The practice of learning from our differences implies that you pay closer attention to those differences, and develop a mindset that does not interpret "trial and error" as "failure."[69] Our differences can provide new information, and the new stimuli in our brains, that creates new learning. Therefore, our differences, more than our similarities, are opportunities to expand our views, evolve our thinking and develop wisdom.

 We *connect* through our similarities.
We *learn* from our differences.

LEARNING FROM OUR DIFFERENCES

A few years ago, I was visiting one of the manufacturing plants at the company I was working for at the time. Touring our facilities for meet-and-greet conversations was an important part of my onboarding. I've always valued the experience of meeting people who live in towns or countries I've never been to before. On many occasions, I've met people who have been raised and still live in the same place they were born. This was one of those occasions.

I was in a small town in the Deep South,[70] where racial divides are more sensitive than in other geographies of the US. So, even as the company's leader of diversity and inclusion, I knew there were certain topics that could be perceived as out of bounds for discussion. That day, I was meeting with the leaders of the employee resource groups (ERGs) that had a presence in the facility. As expected for this kind of session, the visual around the room showed a fair amount of racial, ethnic and gender diversity. This did not necessarily mean the rest of the employee population there was also diverse, but at least the people representing these groups portrayed those differences.

As ERG leaders, these employees had volunteered to take on an active role in advancing the conversation, the thinking and the practice of diversity and inclusion in their facility. They embodied the "safe space" where we could have the otherwise 'sensitive conversations' that could become more challenging with others less engaged in D&I topics. This was what I considered "my group"—our D&I deputies there.

106

Our initial meeting introductions didn't sound much different than the predictable exchange I mentioned at the beginning of this chapter, so I made a point of practicing what I'm now writing about. I encouraged the team to share their main motivation for being ERG leaders. The stories they shared gave everyone a deeper understanding of their *higher intent*, of why they chose to give their time and effort to this role.

Some stories were quite personal, and even though many of them had known each other for several years and worked together every day, the stories shared that day had elements that were completely new for most people in the room. I thought it was quite interesting that something as simple as the respective reasons they had for holding ERG leadership roles was still new information amongst them. As the conversation continued, you could feel the rapport starting to unfold in the room. An even deeper conversation was now possible. If there was an opportunity to be even a bit more provocative in learning from the visible differences present in the room, I didn't want us to miss it.

Right in front of me, across the table, was the leader of the Black/African American ERG, a young lady who had been in the company for only a few years. She was probably in her late twenties or early thirties. We initially connected via email, a few months before my visit. She had introduced herself to share her deep commitment to be a leader and strong partner for D&I efforts in the facility, but this was the first time I was meeting her in person. Aside from her pleasant personality, nothing about her struck me as out of the ordinary, with one exception. She was wearing a beautiful, bright colored African head wrap.[71] After thinking about it for a minute or so, when she had finished her self-introduction in the meeting, I looked at her with genuine curiosity and said: "I've been admiring your head wrap. I wonder if you could help me learn more about it, about what it means to you."

For a moment, the chat in the room came to a halt. Suddenly, I remembered I was in the Deep South. I sensed I may have touched one of those sensitive topics that maybe it was not appropriate for others (not African American) to ask about. And yet, I was confident that with respect and care, you can ask to learn about that and more. Breaking the silence with a bright and pleasant smile, the young lady responded: "It is a reminder. I don't wear it all the time, but when I do, it becomes my crown. It reminds me that I'm a princess, the daughter of the King of Heaven. It reminds me to hold my head high, to wear it proudly, and not be afraid of anything. It reminds me that I come from a long line of women who endured much more than I do today, and that I must carry this crown for others that come after me." You could hear a pin drop after that.

I had no way of anticipating that kind of answer, although I was glad that the conversation led to that point. My *intent* was to acknowledge and learn about a difference within the group, particularly one that someone *chose* to make visible to others. Shortly after the meeting ended, I also learned the *impact* our conversation had. One of the meeting participants came to me and said: "I've always wanted to know about her head wraps, but I didn't know how to ask." I also approached the young lady in private, to thank her again for sharing the significance of her garment, to which she responded: "Thank you for caring enough to ask. Sometimes I've wondered if something so important to me was just invisible to others."

As I heard the word "invisible," I came back to earlier learnings about how, still today, this term is associated with slavery and bonded labor in many countries around the world.[72] In the African culture, the origins and importance of acknowledging that "I see you"—that your life is not less human than mine—comes from the Zulu greeting of *sawubona*.[73] This greeting is recognized as part of a broader philosophy of *ubuntu,* described by Nelson Mandela (Madiba)[74] and Archbishop Desmond Tutu,[75] as the respect and care for each other, for the community. The learning of *ubuntu* is that we cannot be invisible to each other. Who we are, and how we decide to show up to others, is part of our humanity.

So, yes, talking about our differences can sometimes be scary. We might feel uncomfortable about "making visible" how much we don't know about each other, but that is just the starting point. In countries and societies, historical divides and stereotypes create "hierarchies of people" where we talk about our differences, mostly in private, mainly amongst those with whom we share similarities. We often talk *about* people who are different, but seldom appropriately inquire about those differences. It is less often for us to intentionally engage in conversations focused on learning and better understanding such differences, but you can practice doing this in a way that is respectful, insightful and achievable.

You have the opportunity to initiate thought provoking conversations, when you're intentional in your learning about others. It is not something that happens organically. The intent of this book, of the first duality of diversity and inclusion, is to share with you ways to engage, practice and succeed in leading organizations where people are open and eager to learn about their differences, with respect and care. This may create hesitation, but you can do this by focusing on a process of discovery and development of your own ability to understand and value human differences. This will lead you to deliver your most positive impact.

DISCOVER: NO THREAT, EARLY GAIN

When I first came to work in the US, after the four-hour flight that changed so many things in my life, one of the elements that first sparked my curiosity was the Black/African American experience.[76] I knew about Dr. Martin Luther King Jr. and the civil rights movement. I knew about slavery and history and I could have a respectful conversation about Black/African American heritage. What I didn't really understand was the experience of how it *felt* to be Black/African American. Maybe it was hugely presumptuous on my part to fathom the possibility of achieving this understanding, particularly at a time when I was still trying to figure out my own Latina awakening. Nevertheless, I really felt the need to try.

The longer I was in the US, the shallower I felt about my understanding of the Black/African American experience. It became certain to me that it was deeper and way more complex than what was explained in articles I had read or movies I had seen before. I was keenly aware of my ignorance on the topic. Working in human resources, even before I specialized in diversity and inclusion, this was something I felt the need to understand better. I was deeply curious about what it seemed to be a "force of attraction," something I would call a "glue," between people who shared and spoke about the Black/African American experience. They obviously knew the nuances of their shared heritage, the elements of their culture. They would talk about realities they all seemed to understand, but I didn't.

For starters, and as a woman, I really wanted to understand the whole topic about Black/African American women's hair. Don't get me wrong. I grew up in Puerto Rico. We are a mix of Spanish conquistadors, Native Indigenous (*Tainos*) people, and Black/African slaves. My fellow Islanders and family members come in "all shades of human flesh" and our hair runs the gamut from straight (*lacio, muerto*), curly (*con cuerpo, ondulado*), and tightly coiled (I'm still trying to find a term in Spanish that is not derogatory). But understanding the African American experience was different. What was to be learned about "not touching a Black/African American woman's hair?" What did they mean when they talked about "the kitchen?"[77]

For those who are not Black, it may seem like a mundane topic, but for Black/African American women, it has tremendous implications on their daily lives. Hair represents the challenge of "straddling two cultures and the competing beauty standards that come with them."[78] It is a strong connection between Black/African

American women that "bonds them together in style success and struggles." I sensed the need to better understand women who were different than me. I could connect with them and be cordial and respectful. Still, there was something more to it, so I decided to dig into it and learn.

THE HISTORIC MONOLOGUE

As I thought about the best way to learn more about the Black/African American experience, particularly women, I was not really sure how or where to start. How would I go about my discovery in a way that was "safe" and respectful to any other person or group I would engage in the process? I was still fairly new in New Jersey and to my new work environment, so I was careful not to make any mistakes in asking inappropriate questions.

A few months later, at the company's headquarters, an employee resource group (ERG) was celebrating Black History Month. One of the activities they were planning for that month caught my attention. It was a monologue, a theatrical performance that would be held at the company's auditorium. The promotion of the event was not too specific; it said it was a monologue performed by an African American actress. Keep in mind, this was years before YouTube and TED Talks existed, so the opportunity to have a theatrical learning experience at work was still fairly new, so I decided to attend. I will never forget what I learned, what I felt that day.

The monologue took place on a bare dimly lit stage, where a middle-aged woman stood alone. There were no props, no backdrop, no memorable wardrobe. The lights that hit the stage were narrowly focused on the woman's face, not her body. That was almost all I could see—her face. As the monologue started, her feet seemed to be cemented to the floor. Her body, in a standing plank position. Her long hands, her dramatic facial expressions and my own heartbeat were the only things I remember moved during the sixty minutes or so that followed.

The monologue was a theatrical representation of African American women's heritage. The woman on stage embodied the journey of three generations:

- A young woman who was snatched from her African tribal life, shackled on the route to slavery and despair.

- The daughter of that woman, who rebelled the best way she could, inspiring her own children to survive and aspire to freedom, even though she didn't live to see that day herself.

- The granddaughter, who never forgot the struggle and teachings of her mother and grandmother. Her freedom came at the expense of not knowing if she still had a family somewhere, who would also take a first breath of what freedom could look like for them.

I met three generations of African American women that day. Throughout the journey portrayed in front of me, I *felt* the love, the pain, the anger and despair that could only be endured with courage and faith. I *felt* them in their youth, their life and their old age. It was fascinating. Mesmerizing.

I would never pretend that I know what it is to *be* an African American woman. I would neither make a generalization about how they all *feel* about their ancestry. But the quest to discover who they are got me a little bit closer to creating awareness and mindfulness about their collective experience. An experience that still has tremendous impact in US society.

I remember thinking: if that would have been *my own* experience, if it would have been the story of my grandmother and my mother, what would be the impact on me? How would that have shaped the way I feel and think about myself, act in society, on the job, with police? How would that have shaped the way I connect with the world?

For starters, I would probably be on active or latent defensive mode. I would most likely try to affirm who I am and where I come from when speaking with others. I would probably be suspicious of those who are not like me, who would most likely not understand the deep roots of my family's experience. I would be vigilant of any signs of potential repression that would be a reminiscence of what my family had to endure. And I would venture to say that if you pose those questions to yourself, the same thing would happen to you. You would start to understand and relate to that pain and indignity with your heart, not only with your head.

The monologue was an experiential chronology of human beings that I myself would never be. But it was also the proverbial opportunity to "put yourself in somebody else's shoes," (at least for an hour), with the humble acknowledgement that a deeper under-standing of their collective experience would require even more than a lifetime.

The biggest value of the monologue was the opportunity to achieve early gains of knowledge, without any "threats." It was as safe as my own experiment on *Choices of Affirmation*. There was no risk of public failure, but it was still a space for *discovery*. What made it different than watching a movie or reading a book was that I went there with the *higher intent* to learn, not to be entertained. My focus was to be keenly aware of the messages, the emotions and the dis-covery of any element that was new to me.

Think about it… It's similar to when you run through a park as part of your workout routine. Your focus is not on the shape of the trees or the chirping of the birds. You would probably not be able to describe any of those after your run. But if you go to the same park and sit on a bench for a while, to *intentionally* experience what is around you, you will most likely "listen" with all your senses. You will learn a lot more about the *life that exists around you*, which is big-ger than just a frame that surrounds your own existence.

When you make an emotional connection with an *experience* that was previously foreign to you, you open your mind to different perspec-tives. With a world population of over seven billion lives, and real-ities that are not your own, there are bountiful opportunities to bet-ter understand others with whom you share this world. You can expand your view on how to best interact with them and have a more positive impact on each other.

DEVELOP: BUILD A MORE DIVERSE BRAIN

When you work in a global company, there is a critical need for leaders to develop cultural competence - to become knowledgeable of different practices, and worldviews, and to become skilled in communication and interaction across cultures. But in the age of e-commerce, even small businesses have clients, partners and suppliers with different social / cultural backgrounds and norms. For instance, as I was writing this book, I found myself working with a graphic designer in Bosnia and Herzegovina! So yes, it is not very likely that you're exempt from the need to become culturally competent in order to be successful.

Along these lines, in their book about transglobal leadership, Sharkey, Razi, Cooke, and Barge establish that the optimal leader profile in today's global economy requires an "amalgamation of **diverse types of intelligence**."[79] In addition to (cognitive) intelligence quotient (IQ), they emphasize that strong leaders combine five additional levels of intelligence: emotional intelligence (EI), business intelligence (BI), cultural intelligence (CI), global intelligence (GI) and moral intelligence (MI).

So how do you become this kind of leader? How do you develop a more **"diverse brain"?** You can certainly gain a lot from personal and individualized learning, such as reading books like this one. But integrating someone else's interpretation of the same information you've learned is not the same as allowing what you've learned to change you. For example: my experience of the *historic monologue* was eye opening. It helped me see things very differently, but still - my interpretation of what I learned that day was personal. It did not include the perspective of others who, based on their life experience, could have a very different interpretation of the story I heard that day.

The experience gathered from books,
though often valuable, is but the nature of learning,
whereas the experience gained from actual life
is of the nature of wisdom.
—Samuel Smiles

That is why developing a more diverse brain requires the personal interaction and understanding of the experiences and perspectives of others. But let's face it: that is when the *fear factor* may kick in. Learning from and through the experience of others can sometimes be uncomfortable. It can make your own thinking vulnerable in the presence of other ways of thinking. It can create conflict. It can unintentionally offend somebody. To understand how you can develop a more diverse brain, let's discuss how you can manage that fear factor.

Psychiatry studies suggest that a major factor in how we experience fear has to do with *context*.[80] For example: You may be someone who enjoys scary movies. You probably experience them as exciting, because there is no real threat in them for you. In contrast, if you're walking through a dark alley at night and someone starts following you, you quickly perceive a risk, a threat from which you want to flee.

Depending on the context in which you may have seen or experienced discussions about diversity and inclusion, you may perceive them as potential risks, or as learning opportunities. Perhaps you have been in a work environment that does not create safe spaces to ask difficult questions about human differences. A safe space for learning about differences is like the huddle, that "circle of trust" I described in Chapter 3. It's the environment where a team gathers to ask difficult questions, and to discuss a game plan where they all win. If you have been in a work environment that does not create safe spaces to ask difficult questions about human differences, you could be thinking something like the following:

- "This is risky. People have forever been at war because of their different values, race, beliefs and many other things. There is no way that is going to change any time soon."

- "People get easily offended these days. Who wants to spend time digging into differences that divide us?"

- "I don't need to risk my career by being politically incorrect, misinterpreted, get in trouble with Human Resources or the Legal department, or become the public news of the day."

If you're in a safe work environment, you trust the opportunity to share some vulnerabilities, knowing that the *higher intent* is to learn and become a better leader. Having a safe space for learning makes a big difference between being completely afraid or risk-averse, and feeling the "learner's rush" to develop the *diverse intelligence* necessary to become a more effective leader.

So, if you're leading or championing D&I efforts in your company:

- How do you motivate people to learn about human differences, without making it a "mandatory training"?

- How do you create opportunities for people to discuss differences without feeling offended or triggered?

If you're leading your own team:

- How do you minimize the instances where people may "say the wrong thing" or "offend other people"?

- How do you discover the launch points where people feel safe discussing differences, and what are "no go" zones where conversations about certain topics may be non-negotiable?

CURIOSITY, MOTIVATION, AND SAFETY

As children, we are all curious—about dinosaurs and bugs, nature, astronomy, the ocean and an infinite number of things, but life experiences either support, ignore, or kill that natural response to the world around us. The good news is that curiosity can be reawakened.

According to Ian Leslie, a UK based author, journalist and speaker, curiosity is "a combination of intelligence, persistence, and hunger for novelty, all wrapped up in one."[81] However, we also know that a blend of intelligence, persistence and a hunger for novelty is heavily influenced by two elements: **motivation** and **safety**.

If you're motivated by social justice, cultural values, power, profits, status, prestige, family, faith, collaboration, art, music, theatre or sports, that motivation precedes your actual disposition to explore, to be curious about that particular topic. We all come from different places, different backgrounds and different motivations. Coming from your own motivation as your starting point, the path to learn, understand and value our differences is one we can share together.

If your main motivation to understand and find the value of human differences is to appeal to a more diverse set of customers, that is ok. If your motivation is that you want to have the prestige of being the most culturally competent leader, that is ok. If your motivation is to figure out how to think and feel about others who are different from you, so you can explain it to your second-grade child, that is ok as well. It is not about judging which motives are "worthier" than others. Be honest to yourself and "own" your motivation. Just make sure your motivation is rooted in understanding and finding the value of those human differences, not on finding reasons or validation for what you may perceive that makes you better or superior to others. This is about understanding, not judging.

When studying the role of **safety** in our curiosity, Moritz M. Daum, from the Psychology and Neuroscience Center at the University of Zurich, points out that at a very early age, "children trust their parents and primary caregivers as reliable sources of information, who provide a safe base for the curious exploration of the world."[82] As adults, "a form of sustained curiosity, is more likely to develop within a high-quality social network, where a curious individual receives the **social support** to approach novel learning opportunities as often as possible."

The opposite of that high-quality social support is an environment where curiosity is stifled by anxiety and fear: fear to fail, fear to say something inappropriate, fear of offending someone. Dr. R. Alison, assistant professor of psychiatry and behavioral sciences at Duke University indicates that "anxiety systems clamp down" our ability to exhibit the "playful curiosity" we want to enable.[83]

Considering their life experiences and beliefs, there are also people who would have to travel a longer road to even consider the possibility of getting curious about others who are not like them. I'm referring to people who live in the extreme of hatred for those who are different, because of their race, sexual orientation, religion, and so on.

As a practitioner of D&I, I have learned to spend less energy on people who are in that stage, and more with people who seem to be "neutral" or silent on matters of diversity and inclusion. When someone does not show the engagement you expect in D&I, rather than concluding they are not supportive of D&I efforts, you can take a different approach: seek to understand what *would* **motivate** them to get **curious** about it, and ensure you create a **safe environment** for the playful exploration of human differences.

To develop a safe environment, one where people are motivated to get curious about human differences, there are three objectives you must focus on: overcome the fear factor, build personal connections, and develop trust. Let's look at some examples.

OVERCOME THE FEAR FACTOR

People had voluntarily signed up to be part of a learning experience I was facilitating for our HR Department. It was designed to create a safe space where colleagues could learn about human differences. People could pose questions about any dimension of human differences they wanted to learn more about, or that made them feel uncomfortable.

We were a group of roughly eight people. As she introduced herself in the session, this was the way one of our colleagues spoke about her decision to join the conversation:

> My daughter is in second grade, and I'm here because she asked a question I didn't know how to answer. She came back from school last week and asked me if it was ok for one of her best friends to have two mothers. Not only that. She also asked 'why' she had two moms: 'Mommy, is that OK?' I did the best I could to answer in a way that didn't harm the relationship she has with her friend, but honestly, I felt ashamed. I had not really asked myself that question. I didn't have my own answer to my daughter's question: I'm not sure I know how to think about it.

This is the kind of story we heard in every session, because the focus was to overcome the fear to talk about sensitive topics related to human differences. This was not happening due to someone's mistake. It was not a corrective action. These conversations were part of an intentional initiative to develop from conscious incompetence to conscious competence. We gave people assurance that we *all* could and must learn about others, and provided them the social / team support and resources to do so.

BUILD PERSONAL CONNECTIONS

In a recent Harvard Business Review article, Andy Molinsky and Ernest Gundling shared useful guidance to build trust in multicultural teams.[84] One of their key recommendations is the need to build personal bonds or connections, as "one of the most powerful tools to ease potential conflict" with and within a team. We all know there are different cultural norms about relationship building. In some cultures, it takes a long time for people to build a friendship, while in others, it seems to happen overnight. Some cultures are more welcoming of personal connections and exchange in the workplace than others, but you can explore the most appropriate level of rapport and connections you can reach in your team.

Personal connections require a disposition to engage with people at a deeper level than what we have in typical business conversations or work routines. I'm not referring to *asking* about or *sharing* information that is legally protected or private. I'm referring to information that you consider an important part of who you are, including your family, or activities you enjoy outside of work.

Depending on a personal preference, prior experiences or specific characteristics of a work environment, you may be apprehensive about exchanging more personal information within your work team. You know this can backfire, offend, complicate things, or go over the legal line if you're not careful. Of course, you're nervous! That is why I mentioned the need to overcome the fear factor. It is not difficult to understand why sharing such information could create potential vulnerabilities for you and others. For example: how you manage a visible or non-visible disability; weekend activities related to the religion you profess; your responsibility to care for aging parents. You certainly have personal and important choices and boundaries to consider before having conversations about that kind of information. But keep in mind that people tend to be more trusting of others who share personal experiences or values that help them make a connection with others. If those shared values are different, there's still the opportunity to show respect and learn.

As a leader, you have the privilege and the opportunity to be an example about how to share and respectfully manage personal information within a trusting work environment. Most of the time, I've learned, is that it's not *what* you're asking about as much as *how* you're asking about it. A good example on how to talk about our differences and learn from each other is by using appreciative inquiry, an approach created by David Cooperrider.[85] The use of this methodology allows you to exercise curiosity in ways that *value* the knowledge you gain, instead of judging it. When you suspend judgment for as long as you're having that conversation, you can actually continue asking questions with a respectful mindset, and gain understanding from that opportunity.

An appreciative way of inquiry leads to a more thoughtful choice of words, a more respectful approach to building connections across different perspectives. From a position of appreciation, you can ask questions such as:

- "Can you share something that is unique about you?"

- "Based on who you are, or the experiences you've had, what would be a different perspective you can add / bring to this team?"

- "What can I do to create an environment where you always feel comfortable to bring your whole self to our team, not only **what you know** (your talents and professional experience), but also **who you are?**"

DEVELOP TRUST

Overcoming the fear factor of discussing human differences and building personal connections takes time. It's important to make room for that time, by reminding yourself you're creating more opportunities to learn from each other. Once you eliminate fear, you can develop trust.

My team and I developed a habit of checking-in before we started our staff meetings. This means we spent the first few minutes of the meeting sharing what was on each other's mind that day: If they had a rough morning getting their kids to school; If they needed the team's support while dealing with a family illness; Or if they were looking forward to a trip they had planned for a long time. The "check-ins" opened a window through which we got a glance at our whole lives, and the opportunity to develop the trust to share and to ask about them. That was the case when our colleague Mona said she would be attending a cousin's wedding in India.

As it happens with most weddings, Mona was looking forward to seeing her family, her friends, and being part of the celebration. Her enthusiasm was so evident that I felt compelled to ask: "Would you be willing to share a wedding trip report when you come back to the office? This could be part of your check-in at our next staff meeting." Travelling to India, let alone participating in a traditional Indian wedding, was certainly not an experience everyone in the team would have. Visualization and storytelling would be a fun way to learn about an important aspect of the Indian culture.

Upon her return two weeks later, Mona's wedding trip report was fantastic. Her anecdotes were full of colorful metaphors. She shared photos of her extended family and the different events that were part of the celebration. We laughed together when we heard how many dresses she packed for the wedding, and how many people she met, not knowing they were actually part of her family. Mona's story took us all to India, and back.

I will never forget a cultural lesson Mona wanted us to take away that day: "What it's most important to know about an Indian wedding," she said, "is that it is not only about two people's commitment to each other. It is about two families coming together as one. In some cultures, like ours, a wedding is not the final step after a relationship has been established. It's the first step, where the journey begins."

Mona's enthusiastic storytelling was reciprocated with the candid curiosity of the team:

- "What takes place during the several days of celebration?"
- "Does every family member wear traditional attire or are there newer trends in the ceremony?"

- "What is the significance of henna?"
- "What is the meaning of different symbols, such as the sweet treats to welcome the groom, the marriage knot and the sacred fire?"

As time ran shorter, one of the questions started with a disclaimer:

- "I want to be respectful, so I hope you're ok with me asking this: I've always been curious about arranged marriages. Can you share why they have been prevalent within the Indian culture? What do younger generations think about that tradition?"

Mona was gracious in answering all our questions, including the ones about arranged marriages. She provided her own perspective, and the contrasting views held by other family members, as well as different generations who celebrate Indian traditions. Needless to say, the conversation became deep, personal, and enlightening. We talked about the role of women in the Indian society, about castes, and even about the wealth that seemed to be required to plan and celebrate an Indian wedding.

What was intended as check-in became the most important topic we could talk about that day. The trust in each other, the cultural practice of being respectfully curious and candid took center-stage, and we cleared the rest of the agenda to let it happen.

Developing that circle of trust within our own team was an intentional effort. We couldn't be more different from each other (different generations, cultures, languages, sexual orientation, race and ethnicity, educational backgrounds), but we shared a common goal — to understand and value each other. We created an environment where we could *all* be vulnerable in front of each other. We shared successes and failures, even on individual performance. For example: After performance reviews, we all shared the areas evaluated as our strengths, as well as those that needed development, and asked the team to support us as we worked on those areas.

Yes, this was difficult at first. However, it created a more level playing field, where everyone felt they could be themselves (the good, the bad and the ugly). We could speak our minds and not feel judged, but supported.

DELIVER: LEARN FROM DEEP IMMERSION

Once you develop the skills to overcome the fear factor, build personal connections, and develop trust, you can deliver an even higher level of positive impact in your team, in your organization. You might say that, at that point, you're ready for **deep immersion** in your understanding of human differences, in the creation of inclusive environments. You're ready to act as a true **explorer** of people. Using this as a metaphor, you may ask yourself these questions:

- What kind of exploration do you enjoy? Geographical (places), mechanical (how things work), cultural (how people think and behave), historical (stories of how we've lived)? Any other?

- What comes to your mind when you hear the word *immersion?* Depending on your background, values, or mindset, you may think about inserting an object in a liquid, about the sacrament of baptism or about learning a foreign language in its country of origin.

When I think about **immersion**, my mind goes back to the Latin origin of the word, "to plunge," to go deep into a world of new information. There is a story in my life that explains why…

DEEP DIVE

I was sitting on the shore shortly after noon time. The wind was blowing with such force it felt like it was sand-blasting my face. I kept breathing heavily, which was not helping to slow down my heartbeat. My weight belt was nowhere to be found. The air tank was still strapped to my back, while my regulator appeared to be half-buried in the sand. As I kept wiping the saltwater out of my eyes, I stared at my hands and knees which were bleeding lightly after the scraping and stinging of the fire coral on the reef. I had just made my way out through the top of that reef. Even though that was not the way I went in, my diving buddy knew better, and helped me find a different way to get back to shore. It was painful, but I was safe.

Needless to say, my first scuba dive (which happened without proper instruction) didn't go as well as planned. I had lost the sense of control over my breathing, with a tower of water over my head, and an undercurrent determined to drag me away from my entry point. Yes, it was a frightening experience, but it didn't have to be that way. My fearless twentyish self thought I could immerse myself in the deep ocean, with little preparation, thinking that my enthusiasm was all I needed to mingle with the fish in their natural realm. That day I learned three lessons I will never forget:

- Don't underestimate the need for preparation.

- Know the value of the buddy system.

- Keep breathing!

If I had used that **immersion** experience (before I actually got more than one diving certification) of fear and pain to convince me not to dive again, I would have missed many years of exploration. I would have missed experiencing the wonderful world of water that covers over 70 percent of our planet. So, from that moment on, I applied those three lessons to my exploration of life in the ocean, as well as on the ground.

LESSON 1: DON'T UNDERESTIMATE THE NEED FOR PREPARATION

When you're ready to take a deep dive into your potential, prepare yourself for the exploration. You can develop as an explorer of people, and an architect of inclusive culture within your organization. It all starts with your mindset, and then with your preparation.

For a long time, one of the ways employees could develop a more diverse brain and become more culturally competent was to have an international assignment, or a company relocation to a considerably different geography within the same country. These assignments are typically referred to as "immersion experiences." For the most part, they are coveted opportunities to prepare high potential employees to become **global citizens** for their companies. They are training opportunities for employees deemed capable of solving businesses' biggest challenges.

In alignment with this business trend, global citizenship has also caught the increased attention of higher education. In order to adequately prepare twenty-first-century students to deal with "issues of global interdependence, diversity of identities and cultures, sustainable development, peace and conflict, and inequities related to power, resources, and respect,"[86] these experiences are highly encouraged. That is the kind of preparation needed for leading organizations in a global landscape.

Through the years, I've seen different levels of value these immersion experiences had in the preparation of our global citizens. A critical factor on this value is the mindset of the employee assigned to them, who can act as what I would call *explorers* or *tourists* in the experience.

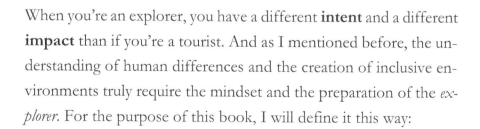

66 **We develop people-wisdom with an *explorer* mindset, not a *tourist* behavior.** 99

When you're an explorer, you have a different **intent** and a different **impact** than if you're a tourist. And as I mentioned before, the understanding of human differences and the creation of inclusive environments truly require the mindset and the preparation of the *explorer*. For the purpose of this book, I will define it this way:

When you're an *explorer*, you most likely:	When you're a *tourist*, you most likely:
Look for **experiences** that help you learn about yourself as much as the people you meet.	Look for **amenities** that help you stay mostly within your comfort zone.
Immerse yourself in a culture or a reality that is different from yours, rather than standing out.	**Visit** well known attractions, which can include guided tours that are typically easy to spot in a crowd.
Prepare for your exploration by **asking questions about the experience.** Your focus is on understanding, not judging.	Prepare for your trip by **creating a schedule of activities** to complete. You might compare what you see or hear with "your own world."
Be **conscious of the impact** your own presence has in a different environment.	May **not dwell too much on the impact** you had in the place or the people after you leave.

Employees assigned to the "immersion experiences," I'm referring to in the chart above typically enjoy a position of privilege that comes from being an expatriate, for example, international schools for their children, social clubs, and other perks. An employee could act as a *tourist* of their immersion experience if they remain within the traditional circles of other expats. They could think they were having an immersion experience in a different culture, when in reality, they were mainly having an experience of *privilege* in a different culture.

Conversely, other employees assigned to similar immersion experiences would act as *explorers* of that culture, by going outside of their circles of "expat privilege." They were intentional in seeking to understand the realities of people who live, work and interact in ways that were different from their own.

Now think about it. Even if you're not or don't aspire to be on an expat assignment, or a company-sponsored "immersion experience," you can prepare to be a more impactful leader, a "global citizen" for your organization within your organization. Consider the following guidance to deliver an unprecedented impact on your leadership potential:

- **Commit to an area of cultural exploration.** Explorers study the landscape and conditions in their area of exploration. What is the difference you want to explore, to know more about? Outline the questions you want to answer during your exploration of this human difference, of the ways in which you can be more inclusive of this dimension of human difference.

- **Allocate time and resources to your exploration.** Explorers determine how long each exploration project will take. They identify sponsors and partners that can support their project. Schedule time (weekly, monthly, etc.) for your exploration of a dimension of human differences that requires the interaction with other people. Get the support of your immediate managers, of your peers, of other internal or external partners (your company's ERG, an advocacy organization, etc.). Identify any funding you might need to make a trip, attend an event, become a board member of an organization that can help you accelerate your learning.

- **Mentally prepare for it.** Explorers prepare themselves to manage unexpected circumstances, obstacles, objections and criticism on the subject of their exploration. Know you will find people who will say you're wasting your time, who might question your judgment or even mock your intent. Remember your exploration may get challenging, because it is more comfortable to connect on our similarities than to learn from our differences. Stay focused on your preparation and committed to your leadership impact.

LESSON 2: KNOW THE VALUE OF THE BUDDY SYSTEM

Similar to what happens when you scuba dive, make sure you explore with a cultural buddy by your side. You'll not only feel safer exploring greater depths of diversity and inclusion, but also have someone to compare notes with as you both learn from the exploration. That's what happened when I met a colleague I'll call Reina. I told her, "You're a whole diversity department in a single person." She laughed out loud.

Reina had been in our team for only a few months. She had moved from another part of the company to take an administrative role within our department. From our first conversation, her professionalism was evident. She was focused, resourceful, had a great attention to detail, didn't hesitate to ask inquisitive questions and was very effective in gently challenging other people's thinking, including mine. I was thrilled that she had joined our team.

Reina also had the most pleasant personality. Every morning, she would stop by to greet colleagues on every workstation near her. Her huge smile (typically framed in deep-red lipstick), her musical Mexican accent, and her positive demeanor made her so memorable that after a while, you almost forgot her hijab and full body-garments that symbolized the faith that was so important to her. Reina was also a working mother of three children: twin-boys and a girl, all between ages six and eight.

I wasn't yet working as a diversity and Inclusion practitioner when I met Reina, but I had so many questions I could ask her! I was clear on my motivation: I wanted a trusting working relationship with my colleague. I didn't want to unintentionally say or do anything that could be disrespectful or offensive to her, but I didn't have enough knowledge to ensure I could achieve this. It took me a few months of getting to know her before I felt inclined to ask, but when I finally did, it went like this:

> I really enjoy working with you and admire the many qualities you bring to this team. Because I share quite a bit about myself, hopefully you know me a little bit by now, but I honestly feel a bit ignorant about things I realize are important to you, and I would like to learn, to understand, and always be respectful to you. So, if it's ok, could you help me learn about your faith, about your life experience, so I can become more knowledgeable about things that are important to you?

Her immediate response was the pleasant smile we were now used to, so I knew we had opened the door to a new world of information and understanding. I didn't have to ask any specific questions that day. For the next thirty minutes, she started telling me parts of her story. She was not raised in the Muslim faith; she converted to Islam when she married her husband. Wearing the Muslim garment was her personal choice, and she was quite proud of it. She shared how she picked some of the garments according to her favorite colors, how she set her hijab every morning, and with a hint of humor, she described how she discussed her life-decision with her Catholic Mexican parents.

That initial conversation was followed by many others. And since Reina now knew I was interested in learning, she became my teacher. Our initial connection, our similarity, our point of trust, was our language and our Latino culture. From there, we opened the door to differences I didn't understand. She would pull articles she thought provided balanced perspectives in understanding Islam, and we would sometimes discuss them during our one-to-one meetings. It never felt like proselytizing. We were truly learning about different perspectives. We developed a level of trust in which I knew I could respectfully ask her any question, without the risk of being offensive. I learned so many things from Reina, that a few years later, when I had the responsibility to lead our company's first D&I Global Leadership Meeting, I brought her in to be my partner, my buddy. With her by my side, I had the confidence to do a deep dive in the ocean of different religions, one of the most important topics we discussed in that three-day inaugural session with leaders from all around the world.

LESSON 3: KEEP BREATHING!

Coral reefs are magnificent formations. They are massive structures of perfect ecosystems, where each organism depends on the existence of the other, creating homes for 25 percent of the ocean's life.[87] The deeper your dive in a coral reef, the more you learn about the layers of life in the ocean: at 25 feet, 50 feet, 75 feet, and 100 feet (my deepest dive).

As you go down into the ocean, sunlight starts fading away. Colors seem to disappear. You start experiencing new sensations. And once you're less distracted by the abundance of colorful movement that you see in shallow waters, you start paying more attention to other details, such as the sound of your breathing. You're aware of the air traveling from your tank to your lungs, coming out as noisy bubbles that kiss your cheeks before ascending to the surface. Your breathing may go unnoticed when you're on the ground, but it's never taken for granted when you're immersed in an underwater world. You keep reminding yourself of that vital lesson: keep breathing.

At a very different time, and far away from the ocean, I noticed my breathing once again... a bit shallow this time, with the feeling of anticipation. I sensed I was about to go deeper in new layers of learning during the gathering we were about to join.

My husband and I were on our way to the farewell party for a colleague who was leaving the company. Although this was not the first time I had been at an LGBTQ-friendly establishment, this was the first time I was a guest at an LGBTQ party, where people knew me and I knew some of them. For someone who was raised in the Catholic faith, I was already quite open-minded about sexual orientation, but I realized that it's one thing to be open minded from a distance, and something very different to be in a space where we were probably the only couple who was not gay. Since I was early in my career as a D&I practitioner, attending the party felt (very respectfully) like our own "coming out" moment, as allies of the LGBTQ community. We were looking forward to the gathering, and very proud to be present at the event.

As we sat at our little table, near a window of the restaurant, the vibrant and rowdy noise of good-natured friendships filled the air with joy. It was such a happy gathering! With music playing, deliciously abundant food, and a casual environment, we couldn't help but smile at everyone who came near us. But still, it felt like one of those times when I would sit still at the bottom of the ocean, waiting for fish to come closer and realize I was not such a foreign animal. I would wait. I would smile through my mask (as if fish would notice the congeniality), and remembered the lesson to keep breathing.

By virtue of being there, smiling at everyone, we were probably sending more than one message that showed our intent: to share, to understand, to be accepted. We were once again a minority that was trying to fit it, but this was a bit different. I was several feet deeper in the ocean of discovery and learning, in a new space for me, and the "majority" of people we were joining that night was well aware of their own experience of being different. It only took a few minutes for someone to come our way and, without being asked, offer to be our "buddy" for that night! "Hi, I'm so happy you joined us! Have you been here before? Come on, let me introduce you to my friends," she said.

I felt **safe**. We now had a buddy who offered to be by our side as we navigated an uncharted cultural immersion. In hindsight, I could have identified a buddy before getting to the event, but she chose us. Serendipity is typically an explorer's strongest ally. It didn't take long to feel we were now a fish who could live in their coral reef, listening to stories that they would otherwise only share amongst themselves. We came in with a **higher intent**, not only to say farewell to a colleague, but to respectfully learn about a community, and we stayed long enough to see the **positive impact** of what we wanted to achieve.

UNLEARN TO LEARN

That night, I started to **unlearn** what had been ingrained in my mind since early childhood: that people who are lesbian, gay, bisexual, transgender, or questioning their sexual orientation were strange or out of place in society. I was no longer seeing them from a distance. I chose to be closer, to unlearn first, and learn something different based on a new experience, make my own conclusions about what I think and how I feel about human beings that for many years I thought were very different from me. There was still much more to learn, but that gathering took me a few feet deeper into my **cultural immersion**.

What science tells us about unlearning, or incorporating new ideas, is that our brain doesn't care for it very much. In fact, our brain doesn't like it at all. As Russell L. Ackoff, author of *Redesigning the Future*, once said: "The only thing that's harder than starting something new, is stopping something old."

New ideas can change how we think of ourselves. New ideas can even damage our self-esteem. When we have a negative reaction to a new idea, our brains will go as far as to block that new idea. For example, if you've never seen a UFO, and don't believe they exist, actually encountering one would be quite upsetting to the part of your brain that says UFOs don't exist, even while you struggle to make sense of what you had just seen. For a while, you may deny what you saw, or you may turn to research to make some sense of what you may now consider a possibility.

Similarly, if your experience through life had been that women were more suited for management *support* roles (some people call it "overhead"), then to promote a woman to a leadership role of an innovation / creativity project (operations / P&L responsibilities) could mess with your brain for a bit. If you have gotten used to seeing young people who are Black or Latino portrayed as the villains and crime perpetrators in movies or miniseries, your brain would have some difficulty considering other social reasons for which they have a higher rate of convictions (for example, that they may not be able to afford suitable legal defense). If you were raised with the belief that homosexuality is a sin, you may have great difficulty accepting the possibility of marriage equality. Yes, it gets sensitive.

When you're faced with changing, challenging, and unlearning the way you think about things, about people, you're also faced with evaluating what you believed before. You will question if it was good, bad, right or wrong, and if a new belief, a new way of thinking and acting is better or worse. You will inevitably judge yourself. That is why it's so uncomfortable, and not something you will be inclined to do, unless (as I shared before) you have a motivation to think in a different way, and create new behaviors, new habits.

> **Learning is not always an additive exercise. Sometimes we must *unlearn* something to fill the same mental space with new information.**

The good news is that the neuroplasticity of your brain has a phenomenal capacity to make new mental connections throughout your whole life. You don't have to stick with old ways of interpreting the world or understanding people around you. But as it happens with any habit (which are repeated practices deeply rooted in your brain) you will need three things:

- Realize that your previous learning may no longer explain your current reality, or may not be relevant to your future success as a leader.

- Be open (find your motivation) to unlearn what you know and replace it with new information and new behaviors that take the same mental space of your previous understanding.

- Activate your new thinking, put it to the test, practice your new behaviors. This will allow your brain to create new habits, to make more mental connections that align with the new information you have acquired.

FROM PARTY TO PARADE

Years after the farewell party, at a different time and a different place, Pride parade was coming up.[88] This was a whole day commitment, not a few-hours' engagement, which meant a new level of cultural immersion. There is so much more to learn when you open yourself to experience other people's lives, even if for only a day! Once again, I had to be clear on my motivation. This time, I wanted to put myself through a test.

I was already leading a D&I team, a D&I function. My job was to guide others on how to do the things I'm writing about in this book: challenge yourself, overcome the fear factor, find buddies, do appreciative inquiry, establish goals to become cross-culturally competent... And because I'm convinced that it's important to practice what you preach, I was about to test myself. This was an intentional immersion into **cross-cultural experiential learning**[89] and check on opportunities to unlearn some things. For example:

- I would insert myself into a community I was not close to when I was growing up, in a space where they were free to express and celebrate who they are. Would I feel odd about it? If so, would it show?

- I wondered how I'd feel about marching side by side of the most salient expressions at the Pride parade, which can be seen as quite flamboyant, to say the least.

- Would I be too much of a purist? What about the public displays of affections among the community? Those don't happen in a business environment, which maybe makes it easier to declare yourself as an ally when you are in the office.

- And, by the way, the fact I was even thinking about the public displays of affection made me feel prejudiced, since I so comfortably express affection for my husband in public places.

Needless to say, I felt vulnerable, but I had to learn about myself, to test myself. I wanted to confirm that I could authentically practice what I preach, in saying to others: "You must expand your views, insert yourself into unusual circumstances to learn something new about people who are different from you." It was an opportunity to walk in somebody else's shoes and immerse myself into something that is so important to the LGBTQ community. Yes, I still applied the three-scuba diving / D&I immersion lessons that day:

- I prepared for the experience by asking many questions about what to expect.

- I connected with my LGBTQ culture buddy, and took cues from him on what was appropriate to do or not do at the event.

143

- I kept breathing as I went deeper in my learning.

The end of my day gave me answers that were very distant to the questions I had that morning. I had a completely different view of what being gay at the Pride parade was all about. Above and beyond anything else, I could see love, gratitude, appreciation, joy, and certainly a lot of pride. Yes, some people were showing off a little bit, but it was a summer day in NYC! We were all sweating bullets, and you can surely see less clothing at the beach. Being a little more flamboyant? Yes, but then I thought that members of my family can also be a bit glitzy, depending on the occasion, even if they are not gay.

I had immersed myself into a space that I thought could be uncomfortable. However, by the end of that parade, I wanted to march with them every time. Each of the nine miles we walked that day was a transformative experience for me. Mile one: all getting ready around our float. Mile two: greeting people who showed so much gratitude to receive a rainbow sticker. Mile three: chanting our Pride motto for that day. The last mile: standing in front of Stonewall and reverently thinking about what being there on June 28, 1969 meant for people who didn't have the freedom to openly say, "This is who I am and this is who I love."[90]

At sunset, I smiled with the satisfaction that I had passed my own test with flying (rainbow) colors. Life is full of opportunities to learn about yourself, as you learn about others. It's all about choice, about how you frame things. You can choose whether to look for the good, the similarities or for the things we might be offended by. It's your choice not to use judgment, to put yourself above or below others. You can choose a mindset that positions you as a respectful learner. People are then more likely to open up and be themselves in front of you, as you can be more of yourself in front of them as well. That is what the impact of diversity and inclusion is all about.

CHAPTER 5
DUALITY 2: THINK AND KNOW

L eaders are expected to make the best decisions, in a timely fashion and with sound judgement, based on available information. But sometimes, the information available is more limited than what a leader would like to have before making a decision.

It is in these situations when they learn to trust their gut, the instincts they have developed through experience. In other words, leaders get used to the practice of "thinking on their feet" and deciding what is best to do at a specific time. Great leaders learn how to manage the constant balancing act of gaining information and working at the speed at which they need to make decisions, which is not an easy thing to do.

This is how I see the distinction between *thinking* and *knowing,* as the second duality of diversity and inclusion. **Thinking** refers to the observation or gathering of data that has not been verified. It's based on conscious or unconscious information, developed through previous experiences, that characterizes what you believe about something. **Knowing,** on the other hand, refers to a conclusion based on verified observation or data, relevant to a situation occurring at the present time. As I mentioned before, this duality is like the frontal lobe of your brain. It helps you *solve problems* and make *judgments* based on what you think (through observations and experience) and what you know (based on verified information).

THE ART OF SLOWING DOWN

One of the most memorable examples of the balancing act between gaining insights and making speedy decisions, of transitioning from *thinking* to *knowing,* came from a leader I will call Barry.

Barry was the top executive of a business division at my company. He had worked in at least three different countries and accumulated broad knowledge about the business. As it would be expected for a leader in his role, Barry would always ensure his team had adequate data and insights for their recommendations, before making a decision on the actions they would take as a team. Barry would act with diligence, but he also had an interesting habit of slowing down before giving the green light on certain decisions. He would praise the team for the work done, and then throw the punch line: "Good job! You're getting very close now, so before we make a final decision, let me sleep on it."

What? Yes, we all asked that question at first. For those who had not worked with Barry before, this could be a bit frustrating. They would ask:

- Why didn't he make a decision?
- Is he not really convinced?

- Was anything missing from the information that was presented?

- Is it that he doesn't trust what we have been discussing?

But after knowing Barry, you came to appreciate the value of slowing down just a little bit—typically until the next day—before making certain decisions. This gave him and his team time to reflect on their thoughts and their knowledge. More than once, we realized how helpful this was, particularly if you had been working, living and thinking about a project at 100 miles per hour, as it happens in many companies. More than once, Barry and others would come back to ask things like this:

- Did we consider the impact our decision would have on this particular group of people?

- Where did we land on some of the questions raised during our earlier discussions?

- What was the final result of that particular piece of research we talked about when considering our options?

Sleeping on it was not the same as getting cold feet before making a decision. It was a practice to open mental space, where Barry would distance himself from emotional reactions, and from previous thoughts or assumptions that would still linger in his mind before making a decision. It is easier to create that space, that time, when you're at the beginning of a project, a relationship, a trip or a big decision. It is much harder to do when you're almost there and others expect you to wrap it up and move on.

" *Slowing down* creates silence in your mind.
Silence in your mind creates space for new thinking.
Space for new thinking creates better solutions. "

or, as the popular wisdom saying goes:

"Vísteme despacio, que voy de prisa."
(Dress me up slowly, because I am in a hurry.)

In his book *Thinking, Fast and Slow,* Daniel Kahneman, professor emeritus at Princeton and a Nobel laureate in economics, reminds us we must avoid becoming a "machine for jumping to conclusions" particularly when a situation is unfamiliar to us.[91] This is when you may have the tendency to conclude that "what you see is all there is." This can be a powerful (and risky) force on your judgement, on your decision-making process. It is also an important consideration in addressing the diversity of your workforce and the inclusiveness of your workplace.

Balancing what you *think* and what you *know* is a necessary skill to effectively lead across human differences, which typically carries elements or situations that are unfamiliar to you. What you think is true about someone may not necessarily be correct. This can happen more often when you process information and jump to conclusions within the boundaries of your own mindset.

Keep in mind that, as a leader, you have the power to slow down, to move from *thinking about* to *knowing of* information that may initially appear hidden below the surface of your initial thoughts about others. This will allow you to make more sound decisions about other people. Decisions that are based on the real world, even if that world is not the one you personally experience every day.

KNOW AND WIN, ASSUME AND FAIL

As I mentioned earlier, in an ideal world, you would consider that your best decisions would be based on verified data. But in reality, we are constantly making decisions based on unverified information. As one example, we might tend to blame one of our children or pets for a household item that is broken on the floor when we come home from work. However, another plausible situation is that there might have been a small earthquake or tremor that knocked it down. Jumping to the most logical conclusion is not always based in fact. This concept is best explained by the *Ladder of Inference* model created by Chris Argyris, the late business theorist and professor emeritus at Harvard Business School.[92]

Argyris stated that we use our experiences and past observations as "data." We then add meaning to this data. We make assumptions and reach conclusions, from which we then draw beliefs / convictions of what we think is "the truth," and then act on these conclusions. This is how you can make countless and fast decisions every single day. The flip side of this thinking process is that it can lead to overreliance on prior experiences and data to make quick assumptions and decisions that may or may not apply to new circumstances.

On diversity and inclusion, an example of a quick run through the *ladder of inference* could look like this:

- **Situation:** You and Anne are part of the Technology Leadership Team. Anne was hired with great fanfare almost a year ago, as a direct report to the chief information officer (CIO). She has great experiences, multiple certifications and several patents under her belt. She is a smart and strong-will leader, and a woman of color. Anne is actually one of only two women in the Leadership team.

- **Observations/Data:** You know Anne was brought in to reorganize a department that has not been too efficient. She has quickly proposed some changes that seem radical to many people. You see Anne working long hours and even weekends. The CIO says he supports what Anne is doing, but he is always traveling and busy with other priorities.

- **Meaning:** For a few months now, the changes Anne is putting in place have started to ruffle some feathers, particularly with people in her team who have been part of the company for a long time. Anne may be trying too hard to make a good first impression on her ability to lead change.

- **Assumptions/Conclusions**: You think Anne is quite stressed out at this point. You don't think she feels supported by the CIO, but maybe she could do a better job at engaging her team in the changes she is recommending. During a lunch meeting with Anne a few days ago, you even thought she might be questioning if coming to the company was the right move for her.

- **Beliefs:** This whole situation with Anne might be another example of what you have heard before, that the Technology department has a sink-or-swim culture. You have felt that way yourself several times. This thought implies that your previous assumptions or conclusions about Anne have now moved to a state of conviction. You have generalized them with other experiences, including your own. You may now be convinced that Anne's job has become a bit overwhelming for her. Clearly, not everyone is cut for this kind of work, you notice yourself thinking.

- **Action:** You've been hearing several people say, "Anne is crazy. We can't do what she is proposing," and rumors that the CIO may be thinking of asking for her resignation. You start wondering what your action (or reaction) would be if the CIO comes by to ask your opinion or feedback about Anne.

Depending on the topic you need to decide on, you may have a tendency to jump to conclusions based on what you *think* about something, particularly if it reminds you of a previous experience. You have an even greater risk to do this when your conclusion seems "so evident" that other people are quick to agree with your point of view. When you see this happen – be careful. This could be an important sign that it is time to slow down and test your assumptions, even when others might be expecting you to "wrap it up and move on."

In the previous example about Anne in the Technology team, you could walk backwards on the *ladder of inference,* by validating information through inquiry. Imagine that lunch you had with her. You could have done the following:

- **Verify your data:** "Anne, how is it going with the reorganization of your department?" She may respond, "This kind of change is never easy. It is expected to have some resistance, but I enjoy the challenge. I know it will take a bit of time for the team to process."

- **Test your assumptions:** "What has been most difficult in making these changes? She may reply, "What is most difficult at this time has less to do with work. It's staying in touch with my family. They have not relocated yet, and we have a four-hour time zone difference. I try to connect with them in the afternoons, before my kids go to bed, and then work a few more hours on weekends to catch up. The good news is that, after almost a year of living in different states, we should be closing on our new home this month. I'm excited about that!"

- **Test your beliefs:** "Do you need any support in getting the job done? Anything I can help with?" She might respond, "Actually, it would be helpful to figure out how to connect with our CIO. His travel schedule has dramatically increased during the last six months, making it difficult to reach him. Do you have any suggestions on how I could get him to chime in on time-sensitive decisions?"

- **Come up with a different conclusion:** "I don't think Anne is crazy at all. I now know how she is thinking and working on the changes she was hired to do. We can help her build connections with key stakeholders, so she can more effectively navigate the way we communicate with each other."

If this example resonates with you, it is probably because it is not truly a hypothetical one. With different names, I have worked through real "Anne in technology" situations. Think about a colleague you've had. Who has been Anne for you? In which ways were you similar or different from Anne? How could those differences influence your thinking about her? For example:

- **If you're a woman,** you probably thought about the questions to ask Anne even before you read them here. You can probably relate to being one of very few women in a leadership team that is mostly composed of men.

- **If you're a woman of color,** you can relate to being the only woman of color in a leadership team, which carries an absence of a racial / ethnic cultural context to interpret some of the unwritten rules / norms within the team.

- **If you're a working mother,** you could relate to Anne and the challenges of going through an extended relocation process with small children.

- **If you're a man,** you may be aware of how women in leadership can get negative gender-biased descriptions in the delivery of their duties. For example, being referred to as "crazy" and "stressed out" versus being a "disruptor" and "committed to getting the work done." This way of thinking has a significant impact on how a leader is perceived within an organization.

- **If you're a white person,** you may have referred to yourself as "color-blind," because you "look at talent, not race." But thinking you're color-blind would be the equivalent of being "bias-free." Just like anyone else, people of color want to be valued above all, for their talent. But that doesn't mean their identity—the facts and experiences that make them who they are—ought to be treated as invisible to others. The reality of human beings is that we *do* see our differences, because "we carry in our heads the thumbprint of the culture." What creates inclusive behaviors is the value you attribute to those differences.

- **If you don't have children,** you may have missed thinking about how the team could best support Anne while she completed her relocation.

- **If you're a tenured employee,** you may have resented Anne coming in with "radical ideas" to question or change the way things are done in your department.

- **If you've risen through the ranks in your company,** you may think that, as an external hire, Anne had to learn more about the organization before making any changes (like Barry used to do), even when she was specifically hired to drive change in a short period of time.

This is how **thinking** and **knowing** become important considerations for diversity and inclusion. At first you may operate through your initial *thinking patterns*. Consider *slowing down* and testing your assumptions. Things may feel similar, but actually be very different. For instance, when you start a new job. The new company may feel like your old one, but there are a lot of differences — in your supervisor, office, culture, and colleagues. This is how "similar" is actually more like "familiar." Getting a new car may feel similar or familiar because it has a key, a steering wheel, and so on, but it's actually very different in other, more subtle ways. Assuming it's the same as your old car will shut you out of the options and features that make it better, or different.

Take time to get to *know* more about a situation — even if it may seem similar to a previous experience. It's familiar, but now it's happening to a different person, under a different set of circumstances.

Once you create a habit of *knowing*, of getting verified information about **individual** situations that present D&I opportunities, you can leverage aggregated data on D&I to identify **systemic conditions** in your work environment. Conditions that may be working against the development of an inclusive culture in your organization.

ATTRACT THEM AND RETAIN THEM

Organizations committed to diversity and inclusion typically place considerable focus on their hiring efforts. D&I practitioners, HR partners and other business leaders engage in opportunities to source and hire diverse talent, to build an *entry door* for diversity in their workforce. We invest in career fairs and conferences. We seek D&I recognitions that position our companies as employers of choice for specific groups. We promote our D&I philosophies, our employee resource groups and highlight characteristics and benefits of our inclusive work environment, such as childcare centers, flexible work arrangements, quiet rooms, accessible facilities, gender-neutral restrooms. These represent hiring incentives for women, racial / ethnic minorities, people with disabilities, the LGBTQ community and other "diverse" talent, but also create a better work environment for everyone in the organization.

While there is a clear **intent** and focus on hiring for diverse talent, organizations typically pay less attention to **understanding and leveraging** the differences they hire, and creating a **culture of inclusion** that drives the retention of this talent. That is one of the reasons some companies have chosen to re-name their D&I function as I&D, to place greater emphasis on inclusion (instead of diversity) as their primary area of focus. But whether you're thinking of D&I or I&D, the practice of two specific behaviors increases your level of **impact** on attracting and retaining diverse talent: *generate the knowledge* and *challenge your thinking*.

GENERATE THE KNOWLEDGE

Turnover becomes a *back door* through which talent walks out or is pushed away from the organization. In *thinking* how to bring in more diverse talent, leaders neglect to slow down and get to *know* how to retain them. There are several reasons for which businesses

158

focus more on diversity hiring than on diversity retention metrics. Some of them are the following:

Hiring Metrics for Diverse Talent…	Turnover Metrics for Diverse Talent…
Serve as a primary data for Talent Acquisition to report their **own functional performance** within the HR department.	Are often embedded in overall turnover information, as **aggregated performance data** gathered by HR **for other business groups**.
Are typically reported on a **weekly and/ or monthly basis.**	Are typically reported on a **quarterly or semi-annual basis.**
Provide **short-term transactional information** (steps taken from sourcing to hiring), which is easier to explain.	Can require **mid-to-long term insights** on an accumulation of experiences/ reasons for employees to leave their managers and/ or the organization.
Accountability for hiring results is typically **high**.	Accountability for retention results is typically **low**.

While companies tend to place less emphasis in discussing turnover of diverse talent, I would argue that turnover metrics and retention strategies should be looked at **first**, even before hiring data on diverse talent. This helps leaders determine areas where the organization may have a "back door," a "leaky bucket" that works against their continued hiring efforts for diverse talent. The reasons for this are quite simple:

- From a financial perspective, the cost a company incurs to replace an individual employee can range from one-half to two times the employee's annual salary. With a 2017 annual overall turnover rate of 26.3 percent (based on the Bureau of Labor Statistics), US businesses are losing a trillion dollars every year due to voluntary turnover.[93]

- From an employee-value-proposition perspective, a company can quickly get a reputation (particularly in social media) of being a place where "people want to move out shortly after they get in."[94] A negative reputation about a company's culture or practices typically has more weight and credibility than the best-articulated D&I messages on your company's website.[95]

The discussion about diverse talent leaving the company is many times narrowed down to individual cases. In the "best" situations, it is about someone accepting a job with a higher salary, a promotion or leaving the company for family or personal reasons. But when referring to these individual situations, we should remember what research on retention has shown time and time again: that if people are appropriately engaged in their workplace, it's far less likely that they will pay attention or seek opportunities outside the company.[96]

In the worst situations (sometimes dismissed as "non-regrettable" turnover), the conversation about someone whose employment is terminated includes remarks that imply the person was "not a good hire" or "not the right fit." Too many times, I have actually heard a manager or even an HR colleague say the person "was crazy." Interestingly enough, I've never heard that comment being made about a man. Every time I've heard it, they have referred to a woman. And every time I've heard the comment, I ask: "Was she crazy when we hired her, or did we make her crazy while she was here?" This typically takes the conversation in a very different direction.

When an organization creates the rigor and habit to gather and analyze turnover data for diverse talent, it can more effectively develop targeted efforts to build a more inclusive work environment for everyone. Data and insights on turnover of diverse groups can help address potential signs of systemic bias that voluntarily or involuntarily push people away from the organization.

In each one of the companies I have worked for, looking at the data on turnover led us to a deeper understanding of how we could do better on at least three distinctive areas: on-boarding, employee engagement and career development. For example:

- For US minority employees, we needed to have a better **on-boarding experience,** not only for the employees themselves, but also for their immediate families, particularly those who were relocating to take a job with the company. Moving to a less diverse geographical area presented particular challenges for those families, as they started integrating to the community where they now lived (you may recall my first relocation experience, which I shared at the beginning of this book).

- The lack of leadership representing different dimensions of diversity (for example, gender, race / ethnicity, LGBTQ, disabilities, nationalities) presented a challenge to the **engagement** of diverse talent. When people don't see mid-level managers or senior executives who can connect with their cultural nuances and queues, they question the value

161

that the organization sees in them, for who they are and even what they do for the organization. Understandably, they will then question the organization's integrity and expressed values related to diversity and inclusion.

- Women in technology who had less-traditional career paths (other than starting as software engineers, developers or testers) were less likely to be considered for the most challenging and rewarding **career development** opportunities. We needed to find a better way to highlight and communicate the value that alternative career paths (for example, visual and creative technology) brought to the team and to the company. Even more, we needed to address the bias of hiring or promoting for "sameness" (a career path that was similar to the one of the hiring manager) rather than for "different" (which creates space for innovative thinking). This was particularly important to authentically align with our core values, which stated we would seek those differences to drive excellence and innovation.

CHALLENGE YOUR THINKING

Not every leader has the opportunity to live in and experience working in different geographies to get a more traditional "cultural immersion." But every leader, every individual, can certainly find opportunities for immersion learning (such as my experience from party to parade with the LGBTQ community). You just have to find the motivation to challenge your thinking about the different perspectives we work so hard to attract and hire.

Let me share with you the stories of the Creative Disruptors and the Mission-Driven Talent, a few examples of immersion experiences that helped other leaders and I verify our observations, and move from *thinking* to *knowing*, from *intent* to *impact*.

THE CREATIVE DISRUPTORS

One of the best examples of "challenging your thinking" through immersion happened with Edward and Victor. Edward was a long-tenured executive in our company, and Victor had been in the organization for almost three years.

It was the second or third time that Edward heard Victor say it: that his department was "hiring for diversity, but rewarding for conformity." Victor had specific ideas on how we could creatively disrupt the products and services we offered to our customers, but had become increasingly frustrated by what he experienced as a slow pace for executing on, or even exploring, some of those ideas. Edward knew that Victor's experiences and different perspectives were the main reason he was hired at the company. So, when he heard Victor talk about diversity and conformity, he paid attention.

"Come with us to the conference. You will see, you will hear what I'm talking about." With these words, Victor appealed to Edward's motivation to know more about the cultural differences he was referring to—the ones not being included in his day-to-day work. Edward made the commitment, and joined us at one of the main conferences of Latino professionals in our industry.

At first, I think Edward was a bit hesitant about Victor's observations, but he used his time at the conference very wisely. He actively listened to the speakers and engaged in conversations with professionals from our own company, other partners and even competitors. The information, the formal and informal conversations that took place at that conference gave Edward an "immersion experience" in a cultural context that was different from his own. It gave him the opportunity to challenge his thinking and get to really know about the systemic ways in which different perspectives were not being included in our company, and even more, in our industry.

A few months after the conference, Edward had an opening in his department. Victor was promoted to the new role, with the support to implement his ideas and a talented team reporting to him. Both Victor and Edward were then positioned to accelerate the impact of creative disruption that differentiates the best companies from the rest.

THE MISSION-DRIVEN TALENT

As a leader, I've also had memorable opportunities to challenge my own thinking. One of them was a remarkable experience that forever expanded my views on the kind of jobs a veteran can do after leaving the military. This is how it started...

The abrupt and instantaneous pull of "the trap" meant that our plane (a Carrier Onboard Delivery, or COD) had successfully hooked one of the arresting wires on the flight deck. Inside the plane, I was still wearing a Navy safety cranial helmet, gigantic goggles and a tight vest that securely strapped me to the plane seat. The roar of this floating city, navigating in the middle of the ocean, was the signal that it was time to release my seat's buckle. We were now onboard the *USS Ronald Reagan*.[97]

This was the beginning of a 24-hour experience of living and working on a nuclear aircraft carrier. Twice a year, a few executives in our company were offered this opportunity. I was invited to be a part of it, and immediately accepted. This was a Navy outreach effort to give business leaders (with no military service) an experience to broaden their views about the jobs and levels of responsibility veterans could take on when they transition out of the military.

One of my first "aha" moments was the realization that this floating city with nuclear weapons was mainly run by teenagers, or at least people in their early twenties. I should have known better, since one of my own sons enlisted in the military a few weeks before his eighteenth birthday, but still… There seemed to be an endless number of young people there, who were probably on curfew and borrowing mom or dad's car a year or even a few months before, who were now responsible, in so many ways, for running this ship.

Those working on the flight deck were easily identified by the bright colors of the long-sleeved tee shirts they wore. Each color was a visual sign of the duties they were there to perform—to securely catapult or arrest the flight of military planes on the relatively small runway that was the flight deck. Every day, dozens of airplanes would come and go, driven by the signals of these bright colored-shirt sailors.

Off the flight deck, there were sailors working on all kinds of jobs: wellness and fitness, including a medical section and a surgical room; internal communications, using all kinds of multimedia to keep shipmates engaged and motivated; food and beverage, to ensure nutritious and diverse menus were served every day; ship (facilities) maintenance, to keep this floating city in top working condition. Not only were they doing a huge variety of jobs, they all needed to perform at a certain level, a military standard, where "good" is not necessarily "good enough." Precision and adherence to standards of performance is the norm. They are expected to "never take away from a regulation, but add to it," which drives a commitment to enhance their own performance and ensure all improvements are communicated to others performing similar duties.

As it was explained to me by several non-commissioned officers, leadership in the military is interpreted as being ultimately responsible for the lives and livelihoods of those who report to them. It is their duty to be "in the lives" of those who rely on their leadership, to know them personally and tend to their strength and their physical, mental, and emotional well-being. For them, there is no other way of leading but to build personal connections with those under their command.

What I already knew coming into this experience, as probably you do as well, is that language—translating military experience in civilian terminology—is one of the main barriers in qualifying veterans for jobs outside the military.[98] I've always found this to be quite ironic since, for better or worse, much of the core terminology—

strategy, tactics, operations, execution, and so on—and management practices used in corporate America actually originated in the military.

As stated recently in an SHRM publication from retired Lieutenant Colonel US Marine Corps Justin Constantine,[99] there were at least three realizations about this mission-driven talent pool that became crystal-clear to me:

- **The remarkable abundance of transferable skills and experiences.** Of all active duty military, only 14 percent are combat specialists. Nearly nine in ten military occupations are directly linked to civilian jobs. In essence, you can find qualified veterans for a very broad range of jobs you would have available in almost any company.

- **The armed forces have become increasingly diverse.** Similar to the focus on gender equality in business, the military has increasingly seen women gain more access to combat experience and leadership roles. From a racial / ethnic standpoint, the percentage of Latino / Hispanic service members has increased by 33 percent over the last decade. And at 17 percent of active duty military, African Americans aged 18 to 44 have a 4 percent higher representation in the military than in the US population (which is 13%).

- **Veterans are required to be agile and autonomous.** While the military has ranks and hierarchy, veterans are given objectives to accomplish their mission, not a "laundry list of specific tasks" to do. They are expected to carry them within a core set of values and integrity. This is basically the same thing you would most likely expect from any employee in your organization.

While I have always been an advocate for veterans—as a D&I professional and a veteran's mother—coming out of the immersion experience at the *USS Ronald Reagan,* gave me a broader and deeper understanding of the jobs that I *thought* they could do in our company. The insights gathered during this immersion experience gave me practical knowledge to counter some of the prejudices veterans experience when transitioning out of the military.[100] *Knowing* (not only *thinking*) how they applied their skills and competencies gave me the ability to legitimately challenge the thinking of others as well. This resulted in expanded sourcing and hiring strategies we could use to attract veterans to an even broader range of jobs. From our *intent* to be a veteran-friendly organization, we moved to a more positive *impact* in being a veteran-ready organization.

CHAPTER 6
DUALITY 3: PAIN AND POSSIBILITY

Do you prefer the carrot or the stick approach to change?

You probably know people who decided to improve their physical health and wellbeing as a result of a painful or scary experience (a stick): having heart failure, being diagnosed with diabetes, or some other chronic condition. A painful or negative experience can motivate people to take actions that mitigate negative consequences on their health better than simple awareness or education.

On the other hand, some people are motivated to train and get physically conditioned as a preamble to realize something they would like to see happen (the carrot approach). This could be the possibility of running a marathon, winning a tournament or beating a personal record of their own performance.

As a leader, what drives you to take action on diversity and inclusion? Is it pain or possibility?

- You're driven by *pain* (think about it as "pain mitigation") if you're more inclined to take actions that **prevent the painful experience** of inequality, discrimination or violence that you or your community have felt before. This can also be the case if you're inclined to **mitigate or avoid negative consequences** (legal consequences, negative reputation consequences) for your organization. You may also be motivated by pain (mitigation) when your organization is still at an early stage of diversity and inclusion, and/ or because you have made your pain your personal mission for D&I.

- Or you can be driven by *possibility*, if your main motivation is to **achieve positive and unprecedented impact.** This happens when you're more focused on **imagining and building** a work environment that goes beyond what others expect or think it's possible. This could happen when your organization is at a more mature stage of diversity and inclusion, and/ or because you have moved beyond your pain and have a broader mission for D&I.

Maybe you say that both pain and possibility are driving your engagement in diversity and inclusion. If that is the case, think about which of the two comes to mind **first.** Which one is your more natural (and honest) intent to drive or engage in D&I?

Remember, I'm comparing this duality to the *parietal lobe* of your brain. The parietal lobe controls your *orientation* and processes your *sensations*. For example: If your main motivation is "pain mitigation" on any "D&I issues," the orientation of your D&I actions and behaviors may look and feel different than if you're focused on a higher aspiration or impact. They will also be "sensed" by other people in the organization. Your motivations will have an impact on how you come across as a leader, and on team dynamics generated by your D&I efforts. Let me unwrap the importance and challenge around this duality.

WHEN YOU'RE MOTIVATED BY PAIN

As it relates to diversity and inclusion, your pain motivation may be **personal,** coming from the frustration and suffering you and/ or people like you have endured due to intolerance, misunderstanding, bias or bigotry. Personally speaking, my Latina awakening was a painful experience that had a defining impact in my decision to pivot my career in this direction. But your motivation to work on D&I may also be about the **business** impact, coming from the responsibility to mitigate or avoid negative consequences your organization may face if it doesn't address D&I issues appropriately.

When you think about it with true authenticity, you know that both your personal and business motives are important. While I would personally love it if everyone would be "aspirational" in their motivation to advance diversity and inclusion, the reality is that people change for *their* own reasons (and motivations), not for someone else's reasons. For example:

- A female leader who is a personal advocate for other women in the organization may become judgmental of other female leaders who, while supportive of women's advancement, may not be as engaged in D&I initiatives as they are. When you start from a judging standpoint, you move away from the opportunity to truly understand someone else's motives, which could help you build a different path to seek their engagement.

- As a D&I practitioner, you may be having a challenging time convincing your labor attorney of having a broader distribution of D&I metrics within the organization. Even though the attorney may be an ally of the D&I work, their main "motivation" (and responsibility) is to mitigate risk (pain) for the organization, in the event the information is misused or misconstrued. When you focus on understanding what each is trying to accomplish, you put yourself in a position to complement each other, to find common ground on how to best increase transparency of and accountability for D&I metrics.

Therefore, as a person or as a leader, if your main reason to engage or support the work of D&I is to mitigate pain for the organization, or abide by your company's D&I practices, let's start there. This does not mean I or other D&I practitioners like me compromise our own commitment to a higher purpose on D&I. But it does mean I'd rather have *that* conversation than pretend you are convinced of a "higher purpose" you don't necessarily believe in (at least not at this point). Regardless of whether I agree with you or not, I'd rather meet you where you are. For example:

- You may personally be in favor of pay equality for women, but not with marriage equality for the LGBTQ community.

- You may be supportive of non-racial discrimination at work, but still feel uncomfortable if your son or daughter falls in love with someone from a different race.

Yes, you should start with this level of authenticity to yourself. While these things may not be easy to admit, I encourage you to recognize if your main motivation / intent on D&I is to "mitigate pain" or "realize possibilities." Remember that from this starting point, you can move from your *intent* to your most positive impact.

WHEN YOU DON'T WANT "D&I PROBLEMS"

It is not uncommon for organizations to initiate their diversity and inclusion efforts to mitigate or address "pain" (actual or potential negative consequences) in at least two areas:

- Penalties for non-compliance with laws and regulations
- Tarnished company reputation due to inaction or incidents associated with D&I

When this is the case, your intent to drive or support D&I could be to keep things working smoothly, not to get into any "D&I problems." Yes, even if they don't publicly express it this way, there are organizations for which these are still the main motivations to work on D&I. But even for those driven by an aspiration of "higher D&I possibilities," there is still an underlying need to address "compliance" or "pain mitigation / avoidance" components of the D&I work.

For the past twenty-five to fifty years, many countries around the world have enacted laws and regulations to address socioeconomic inequalities in the access to education and employment. These regulations may go by different names: affirmative action, reservations, alternative access or positive discrimination.[101] Even when these regulations have been challenged, their intent continues to be to increase the number of people from traditionally underrepresented or disadvantaged groups as part of their student body or their workforce.

In more recent years, companies have also become more cognizant of how quickly their reputation can increase or erode their ability to attract the best talent. This is evidenced by recent statistics, such as the following:[102]

- **76 percent** of people are unlikely to accept a job offer from a company with a bad reputation—even if they are unemployed.

- **84 percent** of job seekers admit that a company's reputation influences their decision to apply.

- **93 percent** of people currently employed would leave their current job to start working for a company with a good reputation.

Actually, one of the reasons diversity and inclusion has become a competitive advantage it's because it is increasingly seen as a key element of how talent, customers and even investors[103] judge your organization. As it relates to talent, recent statistics from PwC[104] show the extent to which women and men scrutinized the diversity

and inclusion strength of their most recent employers before deciding to accept a position with them:

- **54 percent of women** and **45 percent of men** researched
  the company's D&I policies.

- **61 percent of women** and **48 percent of men** looked at the
  diversity of their leadership team.

- **68 percent of women** and **66 percent of men** explored if
  there were positive role models who were similar to themselves.

After considering this information, you may be asking yourself:
what are other ways in which you can increase your level of impact,
when you recognize that your motivation, your intent, is to mitigate
pain on D&I? Let's get to it.

WHEN SOCIAL ISSUES BECOME YOUR ISSUES

One of the most recent business challenges related to pain vs possibility in diversity and inclusion has been an increased expectation
for CEO's to express their point of view or take a stand on social
issues that are important to key stakeholders of their companies.[105]
Such expectations come from employees, social-advocacy groups,
and in some cases, even from industry colleagues.

Working with leaders on how to best address these expectations
became a very prominent part of my work in D&I in recent years:
how to respond to immediate social incidents (and prepare for sub-
sequent ones) directly or indirectly impacting key stakeholders, such
as the following:

- Orlando PULSE shooting, impacting the LGBTQ community[106]

- Incidents / allegations of sexual assault and/ or domestic violence involving our business clients[107]

- US immigration debate on the Deferred Action for Childhood Arrivals (DACA),[108] and its impact on our employees

- Incidents of racial profiling, discrimination or violence against the African American community across the US[109]

As difficult as they still are for leaders, these business challenges are far from new. For decades, we have seen some organizations (business and government) become the protagonists of incidents that generate social pressure (for example, due to inhumane working conditions,[110] disposing commercial[111] or military[112] toxic waste). We have also seen them being asked to have a point of view on social issues that are important to their key stakeholders.[113]

SOCIAL AND FINANCIAL RESPONSIBILITY DILEMMA

It is never a clear-cut decision for companies to determine when and how to take a stand on social issues, particularly those related to D&I. CEOs and those advising them must balance their alignment with company values, *corporate social responsibility* (CSR) and the potential impact on their *corporate financial performance* (CFP). The actual result of their decision to lean one way or the other is never easy to anticipate.

The debate on the relationship between CSR and CFP has a long trajectory, but results on it are open to more than one interpretation.[114] Some studies detect a positive relationship, while various others find negative, no or even curvilinear relationships. In a 2009 detailed study from Stanford Graduate School of Business, David P. Baron, Professor Emeritus of Political Economy and Strategy, stated that "social pressure matters" and organizations "need to be attentive to these kinds of pressure."[115] In studying a decade-long trend of the impact *social pressure* has on CSP and CFP, the results were mixed. From an "industry level" perspective, some correlations of interest were found:

- **In the consumer industry**, where products are sold directly to consumers, there seemed to be a more positive correlation between social performance and financial performance. The main reason found for this correlation is that "consumers can directly reward a company's socially positive behavior by purchasing its products."

- **In an industrial environment**, where products / services are sold from business to business, the correlation between the two seemed to be an inverse one: greater social performance / activity had a negative correlation with financial performance. This connection does not imply a negative impact of overall D&I efforts. Rather, the main reason found for this negative correlation is that "responsible social behavior can be expensive, and there are no direct consumers to reward an industrial company."

From an organization-specific (instead of industry) perspective, Professor Baron and his team stated that empirical research would be needed to determine whether a causal relation exists between CSP and CFP. This means that companies within the consumer industry or the business-to-business industry could find results that are similar or different than those attributed to their specific business sector. This could depend on a number of other factors, some of which can be more difficult to monetize than others. For example: the impact on employee morale, response from investors, counter strategies from competitors and non-governmental organizations (NGOs).

Considering the mixed results from this and similar and recent studies,[116] I would argue that most companies (either in a consumer or a business-to-business environment) are increasingly vulnerable to the opinion of general consumers, investors, advertisers and NGOs have on their reputation. Two main forces for this increased vulnerability are the following:

1. **The ubiquitous influence social media has created in public opinion during recent years**. Keep in mind that Facebook, Twitter, LinkedIn, Instagram and YouTube were all established between 2002 and 2010. This created an accelerated and "bundled" entrance of their influence in our business environment.

2. **The growth of the millennial generation within our workforce**. They are more diverse than previous generations. They expect (as a "given") that companies are inclusive of their differences within the work environment, and

responsible corporate citizens within their communities.[117] The mindset, preferences and behaviors of this generation continue to accelerate changes on how companies respond to matters of social responsibility.

What I have experienced working with these D&I challenges is that they can also become significant opportunities for leaders and companies to differentiate themselves. An appropriate response to these situations can build a strong reputation that reinforces the trust and preference current and potential employees have on you and your company.

It is not always easy to determine when and how to respond to a social issue that impacts your employees or their communities. If your main motivation and **intent** to take action on D&I mainly comes from a **pain mitigation** perspective, you may still consider that ignoring or staying silent on these social issues is your best approach. But the times when companies and their CEOs could stay out of it are now gone. This is a major shift in the role of corporate leadership, and you must be ready to step up to it.

Great leaders are now expected to be vocal, take a stand, and more than ever before, lead with character and values.[118] Yes, you may get some opposition. In fact, you should expect it. But that should not be different from the reactions you get on many other business decisions you make every day.

When working to advance the understanding of human differences and create a more inclusive environment, you get painfully reminded that for every step forward, you can see your efforts move two steps backwards. But it is the role of leaders to turn pain into opportunities to be better, to do better.

WHEN PAIN BECOMES YOUR OPPORTUNITY

The marketing and production teams in my company had been discussing which products and services would be most appealing to the Latino customers. Many of them kept saying we needed to consider the possibilities and develop something new for this demographic. There was enough market research done to come up with interesting ideas, but the opportunity kept falling behind other business priorities. We talked about this for years, but nothing tangible really happened, until that day…

We were at a meeting discussing the product portfolio for the new year. Some of the products targeted to our general market were not performing well. The revenue of those had painfully declined during several quarters. Some leaders were still hesitant to replace those products, but it was evident that the time had come to come up with something new. At one point, one of the leaders said that "if we are going to take a risk on this one, we might as well think about coming up with a product for the Latino market."

The comment landed quite heavily in the meeting. The feeling of being selected as second best took a toll on many leaders who believed we would genuinely do this for the right reasons. The decision to finally act on it was made as a last resource, to mitigate the pain of lost revenue. One of the most senior leaders in the meeting finally acknowledged the sentiment, and said: "I can't believe we're doing this. We have been talking about this for years, and now we are doing it, but for all the wrong reasons."

As sour as the discussion turned out to be, it became the opportunity for the team to put their best foot forward. They got together quite quickly and developed the commercial prototype for the product. They proposed a bilingual marketing focus and ensured the qualities of the product had cultural elements that appealed to multiple nationalities as well as first and second-generation Latinos in the US. The product that came out of a pain mitigation strategy quickly became a leveraged opportunity that the company was proud to showcase as a success.

This may be you at this time. Perhaps you have not yet or not often taken the lead in driving positive impact with your diverse employees or customers, but you can now, as you move forward. You can identify pain points of diversity and inclusion within your team, on the way you approach your customers or your community, and help your organization turn them into opportunities for D&I advancement and business success.

Like what happened with my marketing and production colleagues, in some instances you may have all the data you need to make a positive impact, and *still* be waiting for pain points in your business strategy to act on it. In other cases, you may be faced with circumstances that make you accelerate your approach.

WHEN YOU'RE MOTIVATED BY POSSIBILITY

I've had the opportunity to work with a few leaders whose motivation to advance diversity and inclusion in their organizations did not originate with a pain mitigation incident. You may also know leaders like them. Their main motivation is to seek opportunities to expand their understanding of human differences, for themselves and others in the organization. They are visionaries, dreamers, they are the *huddlers* and *wisdom seekers*. One of those leaders was someone I will call Ken.

After the proverbial *Hi, how are you?*, the first time I stepped foot in Ken's office, he said to me: "I want you to help me create the most diverse and inclusive organization in this state!" As the most senior executive in the organization, he wanted to talk about the D&I possibilities for his organization.

Ken's team didn't have any known D&I issues to "solve for." On the contrary, while they were not the largest business group in our company, his team was actively engaged in D&I learning and had received external recognition for their hiring of diverse talent.

I had to know more about Ken's vision, so I asked him: "How would that most diverse and inclusive organization look like to you?" Leaning back on his chair, he took a glance through his office window. You could almost see the thoughts swirling in his mind. After a brief pause and a deep breath, he said:

> I would aspire to have a team where I see more people
> who are not like me, where everyone truly brings out their

best, no matter if they agree with me or not. It would be a place that I can look back to in a few years and say that we made a difference. There are too many possibilities in this state of doing better for people. I probably can't work on all of them, but I can change them here.

Ken was a white man, who had been in business for decades. After further inquiry, I learned that his intent to drive greater diversity and inclusion was part of the legacy he wanted to build before retiring.

Yes, many leaders who have or reach a legacy mindset take on bold or aspirational projects they may have not devoted as much attention to in prior years. Or as Anthony Lopez states in his book *Legacy Leaders*,[119] they focus on "creating something of higher purpose, lasting value and worth." Endeavors or outcomes that go beyond their *personal* achievement, but that they want to see associated with their *leadership* achievement.

Throughout the years, I've found that many times, diversity and inclusion become one of those legacy leadership endeavors. But I have also seen other leaders - particularly those from younger generations - who have that mindset much earlier in their careers. They *see* and they *seek* the possibilities to do better in D&I. They want to create a more positive impact. They want change, and they want it now.

Maybe you're one of them—a leader motivated by possibilities. You may be thinking about legacy at a later stage in your career, or as you start building your leadership character. In either case, you have the opportunity to do some *wisdom seeking*, to think about diversity and inclusion possibilities that typically get less discussion-time in businesses. You may take on the possibilities to do better in areas that still need great attention, such as gender pay equity, the employment of people with disabilities or health benefits for the LGBTQ community. But before they become additional areas for pain mitigation, I anticipate that possibilities of D&I emphasis will soon include more open discussion of topics that would make many leaders cringe today, such as politics and religion. Let me share why I think this will be the case...

POLITICS AND RELIGION

Many of us were taught when we were quite young that you didn't bring up the topics of politics or religion at the dinner table, because those are very controversial subjects. They tend to disrupt, anger, or alienate those who are there to enjoy each other, and a meal, not debate things that don't enhance the dining experience. For a long, long time, that same philosophy has been extended to our work environment. But in recent years, those two topics have started to intertwine with the realities of what you must effectively manage in the workplace.

Whether you're open to it or not, social issues have become your organizational issues. Religious affiliations and creeds also determine your internal company policies and workplace accommodations.[120] And both social issues and religious beliefs play a strong role in politics.

As conflictive as politics and religion can be, it is becoming increasingly common for employees to feel comfortable discussing these topics and how they play out in the workplace. The fact that we didn't openly talk about politics and religion in the workplace a few years ago didn't mean they were not there. They were hidden, silent. But not anymore.

With the advent of the Millennial and Gen Z generations, we have seen the discussion of politics and religion come to light, with an increased expectation to have open conversations that are considered part of living more integrated lives, of truly bringing our whole selves to work. Some of the circumstances I've had to address in the past few years involve conflicting views or concerns from employees, such as these:

- "My religious beliefs are being violated when you accept a transgender woman in the women's restroom."

- "The Government Relations department is scheduling a visit from one of our state senators. Employees are upset, because the views this person has go against our company values."

- "We want to know how our company decides how to make contributions to political action committees (PAC)."

As you examine and decide where your company stands on social issues, what your company believes in, you may also be judged on what people perceive as signs of a more liberal or conservative political view. It has been a genuine struggle for companies to say, "No, these are not political issues. These are company values." This can present a challenge to many organizations, but yet, it is most likely one you cannot avoid.

Having people be their whole selves requires leadership that is skilled in managing multiple differences, which also happen to be differences that need to be understood to engage your consumers, your customers. You're in a better position if you address it as an *opportunity*, by exploring the possibilities to excel in diversity and inclusion.

Companies can become more comfortable knowing how to smartly manage these conversations in the workplace. This is certainly not easy to achieve, but when you focus on ensuring all people feel respected, their political views and religious practice are respected, you're in a better position to prevent this kind of situation from escalating, become a distraction, financial expense or a reputation risk.

WHEN A MOMENT CREATES A MOVEMENT

As I was writing this chapter, we all became familiar with the name of George Floyd, whose life ended in the custody of police officers on a Memorial Day.[121] At first, many people thought his death would be yet one more name on the long list of tragic crimes of racial injustice. But this death was different.

In recent years, progressive companies have learned quite a bit about how to address a variety of social incidents from bullying and sexual harassment in the workplace, to racism. But yet, many leaders still stumble on their words and their company's approach to these potentially volatile incidents. If you're a diversity and inclusion practitioner, like me, you know that in this and other similar situations, organizations go into crisis management mode. We become part of a fast-paced sequence of events most people are fearful to address.

In the first few days after George Floyd's death, companies started to do what many of us have done in recent years: crafting messages to acknowledge racial injustice; preparing managers to offer support to employees; holding company meetings to listen to employees, discuss white privilege, courage, allyship and offer a company perspective on anti-racism. All appropriate actions, but still, for a moment, it seemed this one would be one more death in the Black/African American community. But in only a few days, things started to change.

As days went by, reactions and protests (peaceful and not) started to unfold in front of our eyes. People of all walks of life, races, ethnicities and generations seemed to be waking up from a trance of social isolation. People of all ages, backgrounds and races took to the streets to break the deafening silence of hopelessness. In the middle of the COVID-19 pandemic, George Floyd's death was creating a ripple effect from Minnesota to Vatican City, and many other countries in between. For me too, this one felt different. It took me to a low point I had not experienced in years...

FINDING HOPE THAT THINGS CAN CHANGE

It was not mid-morning yet. I had my whole day open—no meetings, no phone calls. Still housebound due to the pandemic, this was the day I was supposed to finish writing this chapter, about pain and possibilities on D&I. I had so much to say, so many years of accumulated insights and stories, but on that precise day, all words had abandoned me.

I wandered around the house for a while, with a sense of heaviness in my heart that increased by the minute. I tried to focus, and even attempted placing my fingers on the keyboard to write, something that often brings me great comfort, but nothing happened. I couldn't write a single word. I decided to meditate for a bit, tried to find a quiet inner space of peace, but I couldn't. Instead, I found myself sitting on the couch of my living room, with a sense of sorrow that finally erupted in uncontrollable tears.

I felt lost, as lost as I was many years ago, when my leader said that "working on my accent" was his recommendation for career advancement. I felt fear, the same kind of fear I had when losing control over my breathing the day of my first scuba dive. Once again, the pressure was similar to that tower of water over my head, and a forceful undercurrent that was dragging me away from the place I was supposed to be. I could almost see the scraping on my hands and knees. The strong winds of racial injustice were blowing with such force that it felt like sandblasting on my face. It seemed that business and social accomplishments we had counted as advancements on diversity and inclusion for the past few years had just vanished in front of my eyes. And now, society was erupting with anger and determination.

I had given up my seat before, but this day, I was especially tired. Tired from my work as a seamstress, and tired from the ache in my heart.
—Rosa Parks

Sitting next to me, my husband started to gently rub my feet, a tender gesture I wished could have eased the pain of having walked this long road, which I couldn't help but feel was coming to a dead end, as I said to him:

> I'm so tired. I feel a profound sadness I can't put in words. I'm just worn-out. Maybe this has been an illusion, a dream I so deeply wanted to believe in, but maybe it does not exist.

After a long pause, I almost found myself at the bottom of a different ocean—one of helplessness—as I actually said:

> I can't do this anymore. It is pain, over pain, over pain. Why is it so hard for people to listen to each other? To learn about each other? To have compassion? I'm just so sad, so tired. I can't think about the possibilities anymore.

Possibilities were the topic I was supposed to write about that day. But on that precise day, I couldn't see possibilities, only pain. The only thing I figured out was that I needed to take a walk, so I did.

Step by step, I tried to come to terms with what I would believe after Floyd's death. What changes, if any, were really possible? Did I still believe there were possibilities to talk about? Would I even have the courage to finish this book? I trusted I would be able to figure it out, as I've done many other times in my life, but at that moment, I didn't know how.

Step by step, my tears of hopelessness turned into prayer. Then, as it happens so many times, I saw the prayer being answered in full color, right in front of me.

I had walked for half an hour or so, when I started seeing possibilities again. As I looked around, possibility was all around me. Like beacons of hope, my wonderfully diverse community was there, a beautiful mélange of human differences. If my community could value each other's existence, why couldn't the country?

People from all races, mixed races and ethnicities, sexual orientation and religious beliefs, had found a way and a place to live with understanding and appreciation of each other. They gave me hope. They reminded me that their existence is not only a possibility, it is a reality. They gave me the strength I needed that day to continue being part of a moment that created a movement.

¡Ah desgraciado si el dolor te abate,
si el cansancio tus miembros entumece!...
¡Levántate! ¡Revuélvete! ¡Resiste!
Haz como el toro acorralado: ¡muge!
O como el toro que no muge: ¡embiste!

(Oh, wretch if the pain takes you down,
if tiredness your limbs would numb!...
Get up! Writhe! Resist!
Like the cornered bull: bellow!
Or like the bull that does not bellow: ram!)
—José de Diego, *En la Brecha*

After that day, I focused my attention on what was different this time. What was the reason this would not be "one more death, one more killing" of a Black/African American person? I focused on the unity of people demanding social justice: people from *all* colors, different cultures and generations from all over the country, from so many countries. It made this work real again. It made it necessary. I was reminded of the possibilities that can create a better reality. It gave me hope on the possibilities, and the strength to get back on my feet to finish this book.

I gathered my own thoughts and the input of many colleagues, to understand what could we learn about the reaction that united people in this way. This is what I gathered on why this death had a different impact on people:

- **It was a close-up look at reality.** We had all witnessed death in slow motion. As award-winning American filmmaker and director Ava DuVernay so clearly stated, "we actually watched both parties' faces perfectly framed…It was both men, right in your face, right to the lens—one begging for his life, and one taking his life."[122]

- **We were paying attention**. Four different and equally senseless racially related deaths happened in less than four months: Breonna Taylor, Ahmaud Arbery, George Floyd, and Rayshard Brooks. The deaths happened during a pandemic. So many of us had been homebound for so long. So many people, including single parents, families, seniors lost their jobs. Our normal patterns of work, school, family life and socializing had been totally disrupted. We were at home, with less distractions, focused on each other.

- **We went from collective hopelessness, to anger and action.** You may feel helpless about things you cannot control, until you find something you can act on. The sociopolitical environment of polarization and the devaluation of human beings triggered collective anger and action. While many people felt helpless about COVID-19, most still wanted to do something to contribute to the greater good. Millions of people were available to march and demonstrate across the country, realizing they could have a positive impact in eradicating social injustice happening in front of our eyes.[123]

- **A new generation is taking the lead.** There is a new generation at work here—one that does not depend on established organizations. They get on social media and mobilize each other in minutes. This is the same generation that demands companies to be socially responsible, to be as diverse as *they* are. They expect more. They demand inclusion, because for the most part, they consider themselves politically

192

independent, religiously unaffiliated, and interested in a wide variety of different nations, cultures, ideas, and beliefs.

A few weeks after George Floyd's death, many businesses were still in pain mitigation mode—having difficult but necessary conversations with their employees. Even businesses that had previously stayed silent on these kinds of situations responded with bold and, in some instances, unprecedented statements in support of social justice. This decision came even from some companies that, admittedly, have not previously shown their commitment to D&I, and whose support of diversity is not reflected in the composition of their leadership ranks. Nonetheless, every day is a new opportunity to start creating a D&I change. Many leaders will continue to be driven by social media, motivated, or pushed from the outside to take actions that improve diversity and inclusion in their organization, to mitigate pain. But for each reluctant person, there are also others who are inherently motivated by the *possibilities* of a different reality.

CHAPTER 7

DUALITY 4: RISK AND INVEST

FROM FINANCE TO D&I

In life and in business, there are few words that create greater apprehension, or excitement, than "risk" and "invest."

When you hear the word *risk*, you think of situations involving exposure to danger. You may ask yourself: *Should I risk it? Maybe it's too dangerous.* As a result, your typical emotions will most likely be fear and concern. Fear, and worry, can limit your disposition to act in a situation you perceive as risky. For example: A few years ago, I bought a house that had tremendous market value before, but it was now in foreclosure. This could have been a risk, if I had not seen the inside of the property to assess the cost of potential repairs.

Investing, on the other hand, has a more positive connotation. It refers to spending money or resources on something on which you have an expectation of achieving gains. The emotions you associate with investments are more uplifting. They relate to choices you see as "smart and educated," which drive you to take action. For example, after assessing that same house in foreclosure, I was quite confident the cost of repairs would be offset by an increased market value in the short term. I no longer saw it as a risk, but as an investment.

As a leader, you're expected to take some risks—educated and informed risks—but you're not necessarily encouraged to be *too risky*. Conversely, you're often praised for making smart investments, which are seen as a necessary condition for success.

People tend to base their feelings about risk on either positive or negative effects they perceive about risk. A recent study showed that when people were instructed to visualize positive risk consequences, their visualizations resulted in far less stress in the participants.[124] There is a danger to the decision-making process when people allow their fears or emotions[125] to strongly sway their investment decisions. It's always best to take a breath, get some trusted advice from someone well versed in investing and then reevaluate your choices from a more detached, calm perspective.

Financial planning and portfolio investments used to be something I seriously disliked. I really didn't understand it well, especially because my former husband was the one who used to handle our finances. But the day after our divorce became final, I realized I was on my own. I decided to become more knowledgeable about stocks, bonds, mutual funds and any other investment options I needed to know about. And since necessity is the mother of invention, I got into it from square one: I joined a series of investment presentations, offered on Sundays, by a financial services organization.

Yes, I know. Interesting choice of learning for a Sunday afternoon! The fact that it was summertime and the location where the presentations were offered was near the oceanfront made it even more difficult. I would see people heading to the beach, happy and relaxed in the sunshine. They were frolicking in turquoise blue water. I was driving to the dark and gloomy building where I would learn about investments.

This was tough for me! I really had to drag myself to the sessions. Doing this was not something I particularly enjoyed, but I felt it was necessary. As Suze Orman would say: "If you expect your money to take care of you, you must take care of your money."[126] I had to know how to take care of my own financial wellbeing.

As I walked into the small conference room where I would spend the next two hours of my Sunday afternoons for the next few months, I would constantly remind myself of my goal. I spent long hours in that conference room, taking copious notes, struggling with this new skill, and all that accompanied becoming financially savvy. At first, it was tedious, foreign, daunting. But after learning more about personal finances than I ever thought I would, I honed on the two most important investment lessons I would always remember:

- **Know your risk tolerance,** so you can decide how to invest.[127]

- **Diversify your portfolio,** so you can better manage your risk.

Surprisingly enough, those two basic lessons about investment also gave me a great foundation on how to think about diversity and inclusion. They have served me well for many years, particularly when discussing talent selection strategies and promotion decisions on diverse talent. Working with CEOs and CFOs in different companies and industries helped me discover interesting analogies between finance and D&I. For example, on both fields:

- More information will help you determine if a situation should be seen as a risk or as an investment.

- Even when you have all the information available, you can still feel very vulnerable when making a decision.

An example of this was the experience of working with two of my colleagues, Frances and Margaret.

KNOW YOUR RISK TOLERANCE

Frances was an advocate for the development of women—a true champion, a vocal and unapologetic advocate for gender diversity. Frances was also a seasoned executive, who could easily explain how our business worked, how the company made money and how to best negotiate with business partners and clients. She was not afraid to make bold financial decisions that could benefit our business in the long run. Without a doubt, Frances was the kind of leader that makes our D&I work much easier, but even for her, there was still something quite important to learn when it comes to risk and investment in talent.

Frances was invited to speak to a group of executives about how to become a sponsor for women in our talent pipeline. Other leaders valued and respected Frances' perspective, so they paid attention when she started telling the story of how she decided to promote one of the female leaders within her team.

> I'm proud to say I promoted Margaret for the role she is in now. She may have not felt completely confident that she could do the job, but I knew she certainly had the talent for it. I took a risk on her, and it has paid off. You should not be afraid to take risks in developing talent at this company. We need you to take those risks!

Frances' *intent* was to motivate her peers to follow her example, but in a split second, the impact of her words became confusing. Being such an advocate for women's advancement, her statement implied that promoting Margaret was a risky proposition. While well intentioned, it sounded like she was asking leaders to throw themselves off a bridge while strapped to a bungee cord. You could see they were not convinced by her argument. They were basically being promised "a good feeling at the end of an uncontrolled free-fall" that appeared more dangerous than it really was.

With a bit of caution, I took a side glance at Margaret, who was part of the meeting, as she improvised an awkward smile. You could tell that for her, it was one of those situations where you don't know if you should say "thank you" or acknowledge that you have been diminished in front of the most powerful people in your company.

Hearing Frances say that promoting Margaret was a risk didn't align with her intended impact. She wanted to motivate people to invest in talent, to diversify their teams, but she didn't exactly say that. She talked about risk. Maybe it was because Frances' risk tolerance was not as high as she thought it was when she promoted Margaret. If she would have thought of Margaret's talent as an investment she could make, her words would have been something like this:

> I invested in Margaret. I had enough information about her competencies, her potential and her determination. I was committed to supporting her development, as much as she was committed to being successful, so I knew I could make an investment in her.

So, you should ask yourself:

- What is my risk tolerance?
- Am I really confident or somewhat fearful about promoting a diverse talent?
- What would it take for me to commit to that person's career development?

If you don't think you can confidently invest in someone's talent, remember Duality 2: seek information that will help you know if you should really be that concerned about it. If you don't think you're as committed to supporting that person's career development, take the *explorer of people* approach I recommended on Duality 1: commit to learning, prepare for the experience and dive in!

When you start with a risk mindset, you're automatically fearful. So, if you want to make progress in the promotion and advancement of diverse talent, get ready to shift from a risk mindset to an investing mindset.

INVEST IN YOUR TALENT

What would have happened if Frances had built an investing mindset about Margaret? That was the question I asked myself when I left that meeting. That was the day I started writing about this duality, about what I learned from that and many other similar situations.

Remember, the D&I duality of **Risk** and **Invest** operates like the occipital lobe of your brain. It controls your **vision**. On diversity and inclusion, there are opportunities to lead with a vision that *minimizes your risks*, but also one that *maximizes your investments*.

With a risk mindset, you may cringe and *"hope it all goes well"* when you promote women, people of color, or someone who thinks very differently than you. You may see any outcome that is less than stellar as validation of your initial vision: "Oh, I knew this was going to be risky." But when you start with a talent investor mindset, you're more likely to demonstrate a different behavior. You start thinking: "I'm putting my money on you and I'm looking forward to seeing my investment grow." As it relates to the person you're promoting, it should translate in expressions such as: "I've got your back. I'm in it to win it, not for you, but with you."

As an investor, you would regularly look up information about your investments. You would periodically consult with advisors. You would make sure you have an investment strategy for your short and long-term goals.

With that in mind, I started asking leaders like Frances to develop an investor mindset with their diverse talent. To shift from thinking, talking and treating people who are different from them (for example, different from their style, their educational or functional background, their gender, their way of thinking), as "risks," to operating as smart investors on their talent. For starters, they should stop saying to themselves: "I'm taking a risk with this promotion," and replace it with "I'm making an investment on this person," and then behave accordingly. This included expanding the access of women and people of color to special projects and assignments of high visibility and impact—which in many cases lead to career advancement.

This shift in mindset is particularly important, because when being considered for promotions or discussed as part of succession plans, women and people of color are referred to as "risks" or "not fully ready yet" more often than their gender or racial / ethnic counterparts. One of the reasons for this is that they have less access to projects of high visibility and impact than white men do.[128] These "glamour" assignments are opportunities to work for a major client, build out a new team, or represent the company at an industry conference, which allow people to get noticed by leaders. Such projects are an example of tangible and impactful opportunities to invest in talent.

Another key reason for which this shift is critical is because an investor's mindset is an *active* one, that says: *"How can I maximize my investment, now and in the future?"* It is not that difficult to apply that mindset to the investments in the talent you hire and promote. It leads to asking yourself the following questions:

- What will I do to get to know the diverse talent I'm hiring or the diverse talent I can promote? Remember, this includes the need to create trust and build personal connections.

- Who will I regularly consult with to know more about the different qualities and discuss advancement opportunities for the diverse talent in my group? Have a plan to ensure your diverse talent will succeed in your work environment.

A different mindset and behavior can bring you very different outcomes, and a more positive leadership *impact*. It shows the person you're investing in that you care. It shows you're there for them, to support their growth and success. You can and you must become an investor who grows your talent capital. This is an essential step to move from an intent to create greater diversity in leadership roles to an actual impact in achieving that goal.

 Build a mindset about diverse talent,
not **as a** *risk* **you** *take,*
but an *investment you make.*

DIVERSIFY YOUR TALENT PORTFOLIO

My journey from truly disliking the topic of investment to becoming a confident investor—both in finance and in talent—has helped me identify metaphors, stories and examples that connect the value of diversity with business success. I don't venture to give advice on financial investments (there are great experts you can consult on that topic). But what I do know is that what I learned years ago about investing continues to resonate in D&I as well. Many financial investment professionals still agree that "diversification is the most important component of reaching long-range financial goals, while minimizing risk."[129]

As I mentioned earlier in this book, research has also shown the value of diverse thinking as a driver behind the actions that lead to company revenue and success. I have personally experienced the power of diversity in a talent portfolio: the diversification of skills, mindsets and experiences that makes leaders reach their highest level of impact. But I have also experienced the "illusion" of diversity, because numbers, especially statistics, can be deceiving.

For example, would you say that a team or a department is diverse when 75 percent of the team are men, white, from the same geographic location or who studied in the same university? How about a department that is 75 percent people of color? Or 75 percent women? Is that what we mean by diversity? This was the situation I encountered when I met Lisa's team.

Lisa was the leader of a business unit, within a broader department in the company. She is an extremely talented leader, a visionary who listens and learns, who is motivated by possibilities and invests in talent to achieve unprecedented outcomes. Lisa is passionate about diversity and inclusion. So, as she opened the door of a conference room to introduce me to her leadership team, I was surprised.

She extended her arm, moving her hand from side-to-side of the group, to indicate her team. She then said: "Isn't this a success story for diversity?" She introduced her team, one by one. I was waiting to learn about the "diversity," the differences that could be hidden beyond what I was seeing: a group of women, only women, of a single race. All white women. "We are the reason the gender diversity numbers of this department look so good, because my unit is diverse," she said.

It took me a few minutes to figure out how and when I would have a conversation with Lisa. I wanted to help her see that having a leadership team of only women, only white women, is not what diversity is about. For a while, I thought Lisa's situation was an exception, until the same thing happened in other departments, in other businesses, in other companies. These situations, while often well intentioned, only give air cover for others who are not really advancing on their diversity and inclusion efforts.

I saw the story repeat itself, when Wanda said she had a "diverse" team: a team composed of only Black/African American women. I saw it happen again when I met Roberto, who said he had a "Latino" team, who were almost all from Mexican descent. And it happened again, when the diversity numbers of a technology leader showed favorability on "people of color," who were all from Indian descent.

That is what I call the "illusion" of diversity. It gives a false impression. It seems to be positive, but the numbers are deceiving. Diversity is about *differences*, not about *"similarities"* of a different gender, or a different race, or a different background. Going back to the example of finance, if your investment portfolio only has stocks of one company, or one industry, it is not diversified. A truly diverse portfolio consists of stocks from different industries, bonds and mutual funds.

I know how hard it has been, and continues to be, to increase the *overall* representation of women and people of color in the workplace. I have advocated and worked on diverse representation for almost two decades. We must keep opening doors for others who still need access to development opportunities and leadership roles, but in achieving our aspirations on diversity and inclusion, we must not only *see* the numbers but *dig* into the numbers. We must truly understand the raw data, the percentages, and the story *behind* those numbers. When we say we believe in the power of differences, then we must *see* those differences in smaller groups, in the groups of people who *work together every day,* who *make decisions together every day*, who report to every people manager. That is when we can truly unleash the power of diversity, and aspire to the promise of inclusion.

In knowing if an organization is truly doing well in diversifying their talent portfolio, we must look at their leadership team, and at their management team. But we must also look at the team of every people manager, who relies on the talents and perspectives of others to inform their decisions and get work done every day.

You may think this is asking too much, but think again: Even when the *aggregated* numbers of diversity in an organization are positive—which is a good thing—the *actual employee experience* of diversity does not happen in big numbers. That experience happens within the smaller units or departments, with the people they work with every day. This is one of the reasons for which many employees still "don't feel" or "don't see" the progress in D&I, even when their organizations receive external accolades and recognitions for D&I outcomes. It is crucially important to ensure there is no disconnect between what is being publicly recognized and what employees are experiencing as diversity and inclusion in the organization.

THE INEVITABLE QUESTION

In working on diversity and inclusion, and on the "trickle down" accountability of every people manager, many times I've had to answer the inevitable question: *"So what about hiring the best talent? Aren't we supposed to hire the best talent, no matter their race, gender, ethnicity, disability, sexual orientation, etc.?"*. My answer to this is always the same: Yes. I would not say to leaders that they have to compromise the quality of the talent. What I also say is this:

- Hire great minds, and keep in mind that what you consider "the best talent" or "great talent" may look very different from your own identity, your own experience, your own background, or your own network.

- Understand that your biases, conscious or unconscious, (which we all have) can make it difficult to assess talent that is truly different from what you're accustomed to, or comfortable with. Seek and listen to the perspectives of others who can *see* and *counter* your own conscious or unconscious biases.

When you have too many similarities within your team, you must use *every* opportunity you have to **seek and add the power of differences** to the team. This is what will enable you to innovate more, to come up with superior ideas and solutions for your business and your customers.

The promise of unprecedented leadership impact you can reach with greater diversity and inclusion can be summarized in a single phrase. The phrase that became one of most memorable moments of my career—when I coined a D&I definition and philosophy for ESPN:

> "Diversity is about who's on the team.
> Inclusion is about who gets to play."

It's a reminder that you can be on the team, but ride the bench and never get to participate or contribute. You're just "on the team." Everyone on a team wants to play, to count, to contribute. Inclusion is about being given the opportunity to do that—to show the hard work, talent, and ability you have in a way that makes a difference—to be included. To play.

We trademarked the phrase for the company, so it would be theirs and nobody else's—their original D&I statement, that would become part of the fabric of the company in a way everyone understood. The simplicity of these words was something we could all rally behind. We could all understand that sports teams have a variety of players with different skill sets: some kick, some throw, some block. It spoke about hiring (drafting) the **absolute best talent**, knowing that their talents would be very different from each other to create a team.

When you seek the differences that people can bring to your team, you create a "secret sauce" for success. You can reach a new level of leadership impact. It's about making sure you diversify your talent portfolio, with a team attitude that values and includes everyone.

CHAPTER 8

DUALITY 5: PERFORM AND INNOVATE

Productivity is a business imperative, but it's innovation that leads to long standing success. Companies that focus on innovation know that's what will keep them alive as high performing organizations. The irony is that it is extremely challenging to determine how to balance the need to innovate with the need to perform at the same time. It's like changing the course of a ship while it navigates at full speed. You have to make the appropriate calculations, consider the weather forecast and determine how much you can afford to slow down while you change direction, so your passengers don't get knocked over or go overboard. This chapter is about the D&I duality that describes this challenge, and what I learned about it during the past few years.

Remember the example I shared earlier? —when my company debated which products and services would be more appealing to the Latino customers. There was a big concern on how to do this without losing sight of the needs and expectations of non-Latino customers. Reaching that kind of balance was not a small feat. You could feel a sense of frustration mixed with sarcasm, when a business leader described it as "trying to please Pedro without upsetting Peter." While our product portfolio was very profitable, we also knew we needed to change the course to get ahead of the market trends.

Trying to steer our ship while moving at full throttle was not easy, but many people thought we could do it. Some companies have learned how to do this quite successfully,[130] while others have missed the mark and ceased to exist,[131] because **performance requires agility and efficiency**, while **innovation takes time and flexibility**.

Remember, as I explained earlier, you can think about the D&I duality of **Perform** and **Innovate** as the *temporal lobe* of your brain. The temporal lobe controls your *hearing* and your *behaviors*. You have already "heard" (and read) how diversity and inclusion drive innovation. But you may have also heard (and experienced) the "noise" that can be created when different perspectives come together. Different points of view take more time to reconcile. You may conclude this will slow you down—take a chip away from your immediate performance, but that is not the case when you address those differences with a focus on inclusion.

There is great dissonance when leaders express a conviction that diversity and inclusion are important for their business, and then demonstrate behaviors that contradict that conviction. You may be a great advocate or supporter of diversity initiatives and actions in your organization. That is really good. But how are you practicing diversity and inclusion within your *own* team, with peers and others who don't report to you, but with whom you work with every day?

This can be increasingly challenging at higher organizational levels, where power struggles and competition for even higher leadership roles can become fierce and political. But when leaders develop the skills to **leverage differences within their peer groups,** they are in a much better position to **lead others** in a diverse team. This is where D&I become a performance differentiator. Let me share a few examples:

PERFORMANCE AT THE BOLT TEAM

When you think about your career, which teams have you been a part of that you would categorize as high-performing? This would be a team that significantly outperforms similar teams, and even surpasses all reasonable expectations established for themselves. Being part of a high-performing team is quite a remarkable experience. You know it when you're living it. You cherish it and want to replicate it wherever you go. For me, one of those experiences happened with the BOLT team.

While the project we were working on had no specific relation to track and field Olympic medalist Usain Bolt, this team knew how to operate with speed, quality and efficiency. So, we had to name it accordingly, and we did: the BOLT project.

The BOLT project was what McKinsey's Three-Horizon Innovation Model[132] would define as a "Horizon 1." The kind of innovation that maintains and strengthens your core business. In other words, the charter of the BOLT project was to increase our performance. The project team had three members: Esteban, Nick and I. Esteban was in Marketing; Nick was in Operations and I was in Human Resources. The BOLT project was something we would do "on top" of our day jobs. We all had director-level roles, but had very different skill sets, work preferences and communication styles, so at first, we had a lot of work to do—with ourselves.

Working as part of the BOLT team was intense. For over two years, we travelled almost 50 percent of the time, covering all the bases, from strategy to execution. We engaged the most senior business leaders across twelve different countries, brought in external thought partners and established a frequent cadence of communication with a core team of over forty people.

As tired and jet lagged as we could be on any given day, we felt like we were having fun. We worked very long hours. We would walk down the hallway together, to get coffee or have lunch. We had each other on "speed dial" and would connect every single day. While Nick, Esteban and I had not really worked as a single team before, we developed a dynamic that was quite special: engaging, efficient and energetic.

One day, as we were walking, talking and laughing out loud like "three amigos," we crossed paths with Natalie, a senior level executive with a great reputation as a people-developer, and Nick's boss. When Natalie saw us coming by, she stopped in the middle of the hallway, looked at each of us, and with a big smile, she said:

I really want to know how you do it. There is something different and special in the work you do together. You're the dream team we all want to have. Can you help me understand how to create this again?

Needless to say, we were flattered by Natalie's comment. The next thing we knew was that she wanted us to speak at her staff meeting about how to become a high-performing team. I still have a copy of that presentation, and went back to it as I was writing this chapter.

It was certainly quite common in our business to bring together cross-functional teams to work on a variety of projects, where people brought different talents, skills and experiences. But there was considerable variance in the performance and effectiveness of those teams. There were teams that produced stellar results; some got initial momentum, but later floundered in their performance; others seemed to disappear almost as fast as they started. I'm sure you have seen this happen many times as well. So, what was different about our experience in the BOLT team?

At that time, some people thought we just had "good chemistry," but we knew that chemistry didn't just happen when we started working together. We knew that a big part of our experience was something we worked on with *intent*. We called it our "**team speeders**" —the factors we identified as differentiators that triggered our performance:

- Openness about our differences.
- Understanding of our preferences.

- Active curiosity to learn from each other.

These tree *team speeders* generated knowledge, respect and trust in each other.

In our own words, we shared with Natalie's team the same characteristics that authors Jon R. Katzenbach and Douglas K. Smith[133] use to describe a high-performing team:

- We were a **small number of people.** During my career, I have been part of at least six teams that I knew operated at a high level of performance. Each time, the team was composed of three people. Maybe there is a special rule about "three." That could be the topic for another book…

- We had **complementary skills.** We took time to learn from each other, and to understand the "business jargon" of each other's functional areas of expertise. We valued our different experiences, and relied on those differences to come up with our best ideas. We shared a lot of stories, asking questions such as: "How does this work in your area? What do these terms mean? Why would it be better to do the work this way instead of this other way?

- **We were equally committed to a common purpose.** We took time to exhaust as many ideas as we could on how to make the project successful, and from the very beginning, this was a *team* working together, not three "MVPs" trying to outperform each other.

- We would **hold ourselves mutually accountable.** This was not always easy, but it was always necessary. When one of us seemed to be lagging in a task, we would clarify if expectations on delivery were clear amongst ourselves, and if a team member needed our support. We would review and make recommendations of each other's work. We would balance our own workload, including distributing business trips amongst the team to support our own work-life commitments and avoid burnout.

- We were **deeply and genuinely committed to each other's personal growth and success**, and that commitment transcended the team. We had very candid conversations about how we could make each other better. We were constantly learning from and supporting each other. We were coaches, mentors and sponsors of each other—all the time. We would talk about the path that brought us together, about our strengths and weaknesses, our areas of development and the next professional steps we wanted to take after the BOLT project. From day-one, we took time to know each other's families, to celebrate each success and analyze each failure, so we could keep learning as fast as we could. I knew I could count on Nick and Esteban. They knew they could count on me.

What I learned by being part of the BOLT team was that our differences didn't hinder our performance. We focused on agility and efficiency. Yet we took time to become a self-directed team that leveraged our differences and created our own inclusive work environment within a small team of three. That combination of caring and creating was the power we had as peers—to acknowledge, fully explore and understand our differences, and the implications those differences had in how we worked together.

Think about your peers. Take a good look at them. How well do you know them? How inclusive are you when you work with them? How much do you listen? How much do you inquire? Learning, knowing and investing in each other is what gave the BOLT team the possibility to perform at our highest level. It starts with leading yourself, with being inclusive when working with others at a peer-level. That is how inclusion becomes part of your organization's culture. Yes, leaders have a role to play for the whole organization, but we don't have to wait for others to share an example of what we can learn by ourselves. Inclusion is a matter of making the choices needed to have that level of impact.

INNOVATION AT THE FIRST TEAMS

A high level of performance will sustain a business for some time, but it won't keep it at high levels. Successful business leaders know that it is necessary to maintain a disruptor mindset, even when a business is performing well. That disruptor mindset becomes even more critical when future gains may be in question. Innovation becomes a necessity, not an option, when the market starts moving in a direction that is different from the products or services that a company specializes in.

"If you don't innovate, you die."[134]
—Robert Iger

There is no scarcity of examples where an innovative necessity was overlooked:

- The way we access knowledge today completely disrupted the business of encyclopedias, libraries, newspapers and bookstores.

- The way we listen to music or watch movies today disrupted and annihilated the business of compact disks and movie rental establishments.

- The way we watch television today has tremendously disrupted the media and entertainment business, changing fixed programming and advertising schedules to an individualized approach that is determined by the viewer.

So, the challenge is: How do you go from *leveraging* **differences to perform**—as happened with the BOLT team—to *unleashing* **differences to innovate?** The need and opportunity to innovate requires teams that defeat "traditional wisdom,"[135] where the definition of "best talent" *includes* "diverse talent," to exponentially increase divergent thinking.

When you bring together people who have a variety of professional and personal experiences, you amplify the capacity to find relationships between ideas, concepts, and processes that, at first glance, have no connection in the minds of people who have a more common set of life experiences. This is when you think more about getting the ***best team***, not only the ***best individuals***. The best team for innovation is designed for the diversity of talents and experiences, and engages team members with inclusion. This was the experience with the FIRST teams.

Our business was in flux. We had a highly successful business model that drove the company's profitability. But we could see the future trends—they were quite obvious. Our customers were changing. Their preferences, their habits and their behaviors were changing. We needed to change as well, and fast! We were on a quest of being disruptors, before we would be disrupted. We needed to change our focus from incremental or **transactional change** that leads to performance, to **transformative change** that leads to innovation. We had no choice—it was to innovate or die.

We already knew that innovation teams must have freedom to fail, to be able to test new ideas fast, and to have resources available to them.[136] What we also wanted to focus on was the practical application of what we had learned about diversity and inclusion:

- Diverse teams generate a greater number of "out of the box" ideas.

- Inclusive teams *seek* and *listen* to all voices to build on—not defeat—each other's ideas.

We identified the most important innovation challenge our business was facing: how to become the preferred brand for millennials, who would soon become the largest demographic segment of our customer base. We got the green light to select forty employees, who would work in five teams during the next six months, on what we called Project FIRST. People got excited about the project: we had a very clear intent, it would be fast-paced, and it had the potential of creating great impact on our company.

DESIGNED FOR DIVERSITY

There was one common requirement for all FIRST project members: they had to be high-performing individuals, who excelled in their jobs and their careers. From there, we built each of the five FIRST teams to add diversity by design, with as much intersectionality (the simultaneous consideration of a variety of diversity dimensions / social forces)[137] as we could potentially get. Our intent for the diversity design of each team was defined this way:

- Each team would include tenured and new employees.

- We would have members with clear and visible differences, such as gender, race, ethnicity and geographical location.

- We would have members with non-visible differences, such as working styles, extroverts and introverts, and a few other dimensions of human differences (e.g. disability, LGBTQ) that some of these employees had previously shared with the organization.

We had a handful of facilitators at the initial team meetings, to share guidance and set the tone for the project. As the teams were forming, we took time to learn about their differences beyond the traditional introductions. The *"tell us about you… who you are, and what is the work you do for the company,"* was followed by questions such as:

- "Beyond your functional expertise, tell us about a skill or talent you have that you would like others to know about?"

- "Is there a unique quality or experience that defines who you are, that can contribute to the success of this team?"

- "What would it take for you to feel comfortable sharing a radical idea with the team?

ENGAGED WITH INCLUSION

It didn't take long for the teams to generate an abundance of ideas —almost a hundred. Some of the ideas were more of a progression of work already under way, but other ideas were truly unexpected. As we saw ideas unfold, the human dynamics we typically associate with stereotypes also started to playout: Women were asked (or volunteered) to take notes. Early talent deferred to the ideas of who they perceived to be higher-ranking individuals. The voice of extroverts took most of the air-time. Some of our white male colleagues took quick control of the discussion, as if it would have been previously assigned to them.

Soon, the facilitators noticed that we needed to remind the teams, and even help them pivot some of the conversations, to practice basic inclusive behaviors we had discussed during the planning stages of the project, such as:

- Don't interrupt each other. Allow people to finish their thoughts.

- Seek the input of *every* member of the team—in their own time and style (e.g.: verbally, in writing, using drawings).

- Acknowledge those who offer ideas.

- Don't discard ideas, build on them.

- Rotate some of the routine tasks of the team (e.g.: taking notes)

Once these course-corrections were made, different dynamics started to emerge. A colleague from Finance came up with the most creative marketing idea in one of the teams. One of the quietest members of the group took the opportunity to present on behalf of his whole team. Another team member described how he engaged his whole family in developing one of the idea prototypes: *"This idea is something my family and I had been discussing for a long time! They were so happy to know we were discussing it with my team!"*

EVOLVE THROUGH EXPERIENCE

The prototypes were ready. Five innovative ideas took shape in full-colored storyboards, props, and 3-D models. The teams rehearsed talking points and team dynamics, as they prepared for 30-45 min presentations to the most senior leaders of Operations and Sales. They were excited, driven and ready. It was time to unveil their ideas.

The presentations were planned and scheduled. The FIRST teams knew some of the ideas were more 'radical' than others, but they decided to showcase them anyway. That was the whole point of being innovative! But several times, another side of the innovation opportunity revealed itself as well:

- "What happens if the leader doesn't really like the team's idea?"

- "We are already regarded as high-performing employees. Would this have a negative impact in the perception the leader has of us, of me?"

The fear of failure began to kick in. Most of the FIRST team members were at a manager level. But even for those who had director level roles, the fear factor started to show up in one way or the other. It is not easy to innovate! The organization must demonstrate a true commitment to the exploration. Aside from their own professional reputation, the teams were concerned that some of the leaders would focus on the fact that these new ideas could erode their current business. That was a reality we had to face. We were evolving. This was part of that experience. They had been asked to ideate how to *transform*, not how to preserve our current business.

INCLUSIVE LEADERS REQUIRED

A diverse team must work inclusively. It's not only about being different. It's about leveraging and integrating different perspectives, talents and skills. This is necessary to generate high-performance. The FIRST teams were a good example of this. They were efficient and effective. They produced a remarkable amount of creative ideas. They developed prototypes within the allocated time and limited resources, and created a positive experience for their fellow team members.

Many organizations create "task forces," "think tanks," "labs" or "creative" teams to "house" and protect innovation. This is done so innovation teams don't compete (in time, resources or funding) with "production teams" that generate the performance to sustain the core business. Nonetheless, when the time comes to act on the innovations generated, some organizations fall flat on their efforts to transform the innovation into production.

As Robert Iger, former CEO of the Walt Disney Company, stated in his own business memoir, "I know why companies fail to innovate…It's tradition. Tradition generates so much friction, every step of the way."[138] In contrast, research indicates that leaders who have a higher capability to lead diverse teams are able to generate the breakthrough innovation that diverse teams are capable of delivering.[139]

That was a key learning of the experience with the FIRST teams. Some leaders attended the prototype presentations, but gave subtle indications that they were "checking a box" by doing so. One of these leaders excused other staff members from attending the presentation, saying they were "busy with very important things." They were cordial with the FIRST team members, but only offered a few questions focused on objections, not possibilities. People noticed. Tradition, tradition… organizational tradition that preserves the status quo is often more challenging to overcome than coming up with an innovative idea!

On the contrary, other leaders listened attentively to the ideas, and inquired about them. If they didn't immediately see how the business could execute or scale on the ideas presented, they would say so. But they still considered and offered alternative ways to leverage the insights generated on the FIRST Project. People noticed they were willing to review, to evaluate, to adapt. Even when some of the ideas were not implemented, the team members were motivated to offer even more ideas. "We want to keep collaborating with this leaders' team, even after the project concludes," some of them said. "We know this is the path to innovation, and we want to be a part of it."

Inclusive leaders are instrumental in generating innovation and adaptability. Those are the leaders who listen to new ideas and integrate insights they gain from them. Some ideas will flourish, some will not, but innovation happens when we connect elements that didn't seem to combine before. Otherwise, we wouldn't have phones that take photos, watches that are fitness trainers, or cars that don't need drivers. Some elements of unexpected combinations come at different times. Leaders who are open-minded to different ideas learn to connect those times and the people behind those ideas.

But what if you're not in a position to put together innovation teams, labs, or task forces? Can you still generate innovation? You certainly can. At almost any leadership level, and at any time, you can do two things:

- **Diversify your team: There is more than one way to do it.** Use *every* hiring opportunity to add differences that complement the talents and experiences you already have on the team, with talents and experiences that you're missing. And if you don't have immediate hiring opportunities, add different perspectives in a different way. Create an extended staff team, by including high-potential talent that reports to your team members. Create stretch-assignments as opportunities to work with diverse talent you may not otherwise get to know.

- **Be Inclusive: Become an *idea builder,* not an *idea killer.*** Create the habit of asking "how would that work?" instead of saying "that will not work." You may not use an idea right away, but you don't want to squash people's motivation to share with you even more ideas that can lead to innovation.

With a mindset that thinks differently, a mindset open to the different perspectives of those around you, you can lead or even become the next unprecedented innovation in whatever you do.

PART THREE

EVOLUTION AND REVOLUTION

And the speaking will get easier and easier.
And you will find you have fallen in love
with your own vision,
which you may never have realized you had.
And at last you'll know with surpassing certainty
that only one thing is more frightening
than speaking your truth.
And that is not speaking.
—Audre Lorde

As a leader, you're probably comfortable using the word *evolution* to describe the transformation you're most likely driving in your organization. On the other hand, you may feel quite uncomfortable with the word "revolution" in a business setting.

As you read the title of this final section of the book, you may even be inclined to stop reading it. But as I shared with you before, the space between a strong reaction and the next moment after it is where the greatest learnings reside. Take a few minutes if you need to, and then consider the following:

- Evolution is gradual. Revolution is immediate.

- Evolution can sometimes go unnoticed. Revolution creates noticeable change.

- Evolution is **intentional**. Revolution is **impactful**.

That is what I mean by evolution and revolution. I'm not suggesting riots or violence at all. I'm encouraging you to go for more immediate, noticeable and impactful change. The kind of change that you can lead when you leverage the knowledge of the five dualities of diversity and inclusion. Let me share an example that may resonate with you...

According to public records, my home is over one hundred years old. Although at first glance it looks like a new house, the building blocks of its foundation show their age; they have a texture and shape that is quite different from modern building materials. You notice their age, but also their strength. A centennial strength that still carries the weight of the structure I call home.

When you walk around my neighborhood, it is easy to see similar building blocks in other homes. Blocks that seem to tell the story of a different time, when years would pass by more slowly. But centennial houses need renovations, so they can remain functional and livable for their residents.

Some home renovations in my neighborhood have been done gradually: new roof, new floors, new kitchen. One space at a time. That was not the case of my house. Before my husband and I purchased it a year ago, the house had gone through years of decay. It was crumbling at such a fast pace, that there was no time left for gradual renovations. No evolution would suffice. It needed immediate action, a revolutionary reconstruction that would make it a livable space again.

Like the homes in my neighborhood, some of the changes needed in our organizations and our society will continue experiencing gradual evolution and renovation. But in other instances, we are seeing how the structures built on solid foundations are crumbling in front of our eyes.

As it related to companies, people are no longer willing to work in organizations that have the following:

- "Moldy walls" that create toxic environments.
- "Glass ceilings" that let in some light, but inhibit the growth of some people.
- Staircases that create a "nice entrance" to the organization, but have the front door shut for leadership advancement.
- Closed spaces and conversations that people want to break down, to create "open floor plans" where they can be seen and heard.

As it relates to the society where we live, it has become increasingly difficult to see the texture and shape of the building blocks of its foundation, and the Declaration of Independence[140] that so proudly we hail.

We seek validation of the principles of freedom:

- "That we have unalienable rights of life, liberty and the pursuit of happiness."

Of the pronouncement against inequality:

- "The circumstances of our emigration and settlement here."

Of our commitment to each other:

- We "mutually pledge to each other our Lives, our Fortunes and our Sacred Honor."

In our renovated home—of work and society—the foundation of freedom must include every man and woman, as human beings. Otherwise, our home becomes dysfunctional and unlivable. And no matter how we look outside, the color of our facade does not make our house less of a home.

You're the "owner" of a workplace. You have the power and the privilege to make it the crown jewel of your neighborhood. Look at it with a critical eye:

- What are the renovations needed?
- Which of those could be done gradually?
- Which ones are in need of a complete and immediate renovation?
- Where will you lead an evolution?
- Where will you lead a revolution?

You have a choice. You have a decision to make.

CHAPTER 9
MULTIPLY YOUR IMPACT

Instead of focusing on the challenges, and on the risks of change and transformation, you can focus on the opportunities, and on the possibilities to have a higher impact that is within your reach. Consider the following:

- What do *you* want to change?

- What is the impact *you* want to have?

- What are the "big buttons" of cultural transformation *you* can push in your organization, and because you can, you should?

- Would you lead a *gradual* D&I evolution, an *expedited* D&I evolution or an *accelerated* D&I revolution?

Now that you understand the five dualities of diversity and inclusion, there's a decision for you to make: **What is the level of impact you want to have?**

- How will you activate your curiosity to **learn about human differences**?

- How will you practice new behaviors that **generate a more inclusive environment** for those around you?

- Will you **wait for or will you seek opportunities** to learn about yourself and others?

  o *Will you do this at a more **personal** level?* Within family, friends or in individual conversations. These are the private learnings and actions that have personal impact.

  o *Will you do this at a **leadership** level?* In your organization, with groups of people you can collectively impact with your decisions and actions. These are the learnings and actions that have organizational impact.

  o *Will you do this at a **social** level?* In your community, with people you may not even know, or will never get to know. These are the learnings and actions that have the broadest impact in our society.

Once again, that is a choice only you can make for yourself, but be conscious and intentional about it. Don't underestimate that your impact can generate a gradual or expedited evolution in your life and the lives of others, or an accelerated revolution in your community, in our society.

PERSONAL IMPACT

Personal impact is about understanding your individual interactions. It's about making the choice to seize moments when you can have an impact in someone's life, and someone can have an impact in yours—giving you an experience or a level of understanding you didn't have before. This is when you have to pay attention. To be "in the moment," so you don't miss the opportunity.

Some time ago, I was asked to moderate a panel discussion about ways to be more inclusive of people with disabilities. I was excited to accept this invitation, since the event was organized by one of our company's employee resource groups and their executive champion. I didn't personally know each of the panelists selected by the group, so as part of my preparation for the event, I asked the group leader which were the specific disabilities the panelists would be talking about. With what seemed like a mix of certainty and confusion, he said:

> One of our colleagues is a little person.[141] One is hard of hearing.[142] Another one is blind.[143] The fourth one, Blake—I'm not really sure. He said he has an invisible disability.[144]

I paused for a minute. The fact that Blake was participating in the panel would imply he was willing to speak about his disability, but:

- What questions should or could I ask a panelist with an invisible disability?

- Would he speak openly about the disability during the panel conversation?

- Was this something he had previously disclosed or would this be the first time he was talking about it at work?

- To what degree would he be comfortable addressing specific questions from the event participants?

These were already too many unanswered questions. I took it as a sign of the need to learn something important about myself—how to best address this situation—and about someone with an invisible disability. So as part of my preparation process, I asked to meet with Blake.

I had spoken with Blake a few times before, about other ERG matters, but didn't know he had an invisible disability. When he walked into my office, we smiled at each other. Blake had one of those big smiles that brings joy to any encounter. But he also had a hint of sadness that sits in the corners of his eyes. As we sat side by side near my office window, my inevitable thoughts tried to figure out what was his invisible disability, but I made a very conscious effort to get out of my head, and just listen.

> I know it may have puzzled you to hear I have an invisible disability, and that I want to talk about it at the panel. My manager knows about it, but I have not yet told anyone else at the company.

I took a moment to let Blake know I was not asking him to disclose this information to me, so I clarified my intent: "I'm seeking to understand which would be the questions I could ask you during the panel discussion," I said. "How can I best guide the conversation that day to help you share your story? What you want to share about your invisible disability." After a brief pause that transformed into an expression of determination, he responded: "Mental health. I want to talk about my mental health."

It seemed that hearing himself openly say that sentence was in itself a big hurdle he had just overcome. I acknowledged this sentiment, and said: "I hear you." After a sigh of relief, he continued:

> I have suffered depression for many years, and have feared how others would interpret it. What assumptions or concerns they would have about my performance and my career aspirations if they knew about it. I have thought about this for a long time, and have come to a realization: If I keep this fear inside me, it will grow. If I share it with others, I can get rid of it.

What was intended to be a thirty-minute conversation extended for over an hour. Depression was the disability he decided to speak about at the panel, but there was so much more to know about Blake! We talked about the experiences that had led to his chronic depression. He shared the unfortunate decisions he had made at times of despair, when depression led to crisis. We talked about his identity, his family and many other layers of who he is.

The rest of the conversation I had with Blake that day will forever remain in the safe space we created between two seats near my office window, where his story and our tears came together as one human emotion. I didn't just listen to Blake. I ended up sharing with him stories about my own life that I had not shared with anyone at work, neither before nor after that day. We promised to lock the moment in our hearts, and threw the key out the window.

Respect and care opened a space for Blake's vulnerability to feel supported. An environment of inclusion allowed Blake to free himself from a fear he had been holding for years. That day, we built a moment of personal impact, for both of us.

This kind of moment crosses your path every single day. I'm sure you have your own examples of experiences similar to my conversation with Blake. The question is:

- How many of those learning are you *seeking*, versus waiting for them to happen?

- How many times do you notice or become aware of something that is important to one of your colleagues and team members? Do you ask about it? Do you exercise respect and curiosity that leads to a better understanding of others?

Even if you're still hesitant to ask about differences you're not familiar with, remember that by exercising respect in your curiosity, you can increase your understanding and appreciation of others. There is no guarantee that in every situation you will be successful, but keep in mind that the worst thing you can do is not try.

You have the choice. You have a decision to make.

LEADERSHIP IMPACT

In the long run, we shape our lives, and we shape ourselves...
...And the choices we make are ultimately our
own responsibility.
—Eleanor Roosevelt

As a leader, you choose what level of impact you want to have as it relates to diversity and inclusion. Some leaders focus on doing their functional job very well. They still prefer to hire people who are similar to them. They are comfortable with performing and speeding up if change is needed or expected from them. And for a long time, this is how leaders have raised and thrived. But the kind of leadership I have described in this book is different.

You don't just "happen" to understand, leverage and embrace human differences. It's a choice you make to have a higher level of leadership impact—one that challenges the status quo, that makes difficult choices and drives change that has a more immediate, revolutionary, transformative impact that goes above and beyond your expected business success.

You could focus on the challenges of diversity and inclusion, and keep thinking that:

- Building a more diverse leadership team will take a long time.

- The talent pool is not sufficient or that you don't know how to find it.

- There is no way you can please everybody.

- People still need to "fit" in your company's culture, even when you speak about the need to have business and culture transformation.

- There is a lot of financial, cultural, and personal risk in taking a stand on social issues.

You could choose to wait for that gradual evolution that (maybe, only maybe) changes the inequalities in our society. But what about the inequalities that exist in the workplace you lead? You're responsible for those. You may have inherited a lack of diversity and inclusion in your team, in your organization, but you're the one in charge right now. How will you use that power? How will you define your leadership impact?

THE CHOICE IS YOURS

As I finish writing this book, several themes and thoughts keep coming up. There is a re-awakening to the severe and systemic racial injustice in the US.

An increased number of senior leaders in prominent companies have made the choice to have a higher level of impact. CEOs are taking a stand as they never did before. Some of them are personally leading listening sessions with their employees, and thinking about ways to make of this moment a sustainable change. More of those leaders are needed. Will you be one of them?

The level of leadership impact you can reach in understanding and valuing human differences can be achieved when you lean towards those five right-hand elements of the dualities we have covered:

- Learn   • Know   • Invest   • Possibility   • Innovate

I encourage you to not only keep the information for yourself in a safe place that has no risk. I encourage you to share your learnings —with colleagues, team members and any others impacted by your leadership. Create your own challenge of thinking differently, of learning about yourself and others around you. Because if not you, then who? You're the one you have waited for. Be the leader your employees, your company and your industry needs.

- Look around, to identify opportunities to add the differences that are missing in your team. One way to do this is to create an "extended leadership" team, that includes emerging diverse talent who reports one or two levels below your staff.

- Challenge your own thinking and learn from others who are different from you. Be curious, be open-minded. You will be better for it.

- Seek and seize the opportunities to create an environment where people who are different can be heard. Build (not kill) the ideas of others. They will do better for it.

- Bring together other leaders in your industry, to work collectively on opportunities to accelerate, innovate and revolutionize your D&I impact. We will all do better for it.

You have the choice. You have a decision to make. In writing this book, I faced and reflected on my own decisions and consequences. I guarantee you that whatever choice you make, it will not be easy. It will not happen overnight. You will lose people, and find people. It's a process, a quest, and a path worth following.

SOCIAL IMPACT

We may have not chosen the time, but the time has chosen us.
—John Lewis

Our country is facing deep unrest and polarization at this time. It sometimes looks and feels like we are at war with each other. The easy thing to do would be to sit back and watch how things play out before we commit to transformation. We want change, we're dying for it, but we also want to be safe. Choices must be made.

As I finish writing this book, I continue to hear people asking if:

- The movement to end racial injustice will die down after a few months.

- Gender pay equity will continue to linger without more definitive court decisions.

- The rights of the LGBTQ community will continue to be curtailed by executive orders.

- The impact of a pandemic will continue to wipe-out populations that are already impacted by social determinants of health.

- We will kick out of this country the younger generation of immigrants that represent the brain power and stamina that will lead our business and our country in the next 25 yrs.

These situations are not happening *outside* of your business. They are impacting the people who *are* your business: your employees, your customers, your partners.

Multiplying your leadership to the level of social impact starts when you ask yourself:

- What should I know about those situations?

- What can I personally do to have a positive impact in this situation?

- What can my company do to address those social issues?

- How far am I going to take my understanding, my appreciation and my impact in social issues, beyond the work I do for my company?

For the most part, a company's social impact has been ascribed to their corporate citizenship efforts, their support and encouragement of social volunteering programs for their employees and their philanthropy efforts. But much more can be done. Companies and leaders can do more to actively engage in organizations that promote the advancement of disadvantaged communities. This engagement is typically seen in leaders and executives of color, but it is not that common for the majority of leaders—who are white men. This level of social impact goes beyond sitting as board member or securing funds for these organizations. It includes a deeper level of impact, such as:

- Immersion opportunities to collaborate with members of these communities, to gain perspectives you would otherwise not have.

- Formal programs of mentoring and reverse mentoring with students and young professionals in sectors that are underrepresented at the leadership level.

- Training, hiring and providing a diverse work environment for immigrants and refugees.[145]

- Providing meaningful job opportunities to candidates who have had a previous criminal background—which happens to be one in every three adults in the US—to break cycles of poverty that continue to crush the possibilities to do better.

This is the kind of work that has sustainable social impact. This is the kind of work that changes you, while you do the work. You can extend your leadership impact to create a more equitable society for everyone.

You have the choice. You have a decision to make. What will it be?

A JOURNEY OF A MILLION STEPS

Writing this book has been one of the most difficult things I've ever done. It's been a journey of a million steps back into time, as well as the present. It took reflection on the pain and the failures, the effort and the successes. It took courage. It took endurance. It made me face my fears and cherish treasured moments of my life—when I could move a boulder, even if only an inch, to be a voice for others. To break a silence. To stand up. To pull others who wanted to rise and shine, so the world could see their beauty and their value. This has meant the world to me.

Beyond the impact those experiences imprinted in my soul, the journey is now in writing. It can now transcend beyond my lifetime and the memories of those with whom I shared this journey. May the learnings that I carefully picked up along the way inspire others, encourage many, to keep fighting the good fight. Stand up for others, have a personal impact. A leadership impact. A social impact. We must not leave that mission to others. We are the ones we have been waiting for. Pick up the torch, so we can keep moving forward.

CHAPTER 10
LET'S WRITE THIS ONE TOGETHER

I value the opportunity you gave me to spend time with you, while you took time to read this book. It is my hope that what you learned and reflected upon by reading this book leads you to a greater exploration, understanding and valuing of human differences. To become a better version of yourself, as a person and as a leader.

I'm convinced that the next chapter of diversity and inclusion is the one we are writing right now, together: you, me, and every other leader who gets it. Those leaders who make the choice to learn about themselves, about others. Those who focus on the possibilities to innovate, to create, to lead an expedited evolution or an accelerated revolution on diversity and inclusion.

This is your invitation to become a writer of our next chapter. If you enjoyed this book and gained even a few insights that will help you be different, think differently and lead differently, please share them with others. Share what you have learned with your family and friends, and any others who you believe could benefit from this book, and then make it known to others. These are some of the ways we can start writing that chapter together:

- **Write a book review on Amazon** (www.amazon.com). Your impressions and takeaways matter. I'm looking forward to being your reader now, and learning more about the *impact* this book had on you, and what you gained from reading *From Intent to Impact: the 5 Dualities of Diversity and Inclusion.*

- **Keep building our impact with the e-learning program.** If you find yourself inspired to the point of taking that next important step in understanding human differences, and getting from *intent* to *impact,* I have good news for you. I have created a course that goes along with this book. Here is a link (https://di-md-learning.thinkific.com/) to access the first module. This program will support you in identifying tangible actions to reach your most unprecedented level of personal, leadership and social impact.

- **Stay in touch.** Reach out to me with questions or comments about the book. Please feel free connect via LinkedIn (https://www.linkedin.com/in/monicadiaz1/) or email me: monica@diversityinclusion-md.com

Let the diversity of human experiences transform who you are, as you transform the world we all live in.

DEDICATION

To my beloved family, especially my husband Rolando, for being my loving oasis at times of uncertainty and boundless wisdom at times of reflection. To my four children—all born in my heart: Rolando J., Miguel R., Jaime L. and Rosa I., for sharing your conviction that this book would see the light of day. To my parents, Isabel and Santos, and my siblings: Veronica, Elizabeth, Deborah and Alfredo, for your unconditional love and support.

To all of you, I dedicate the memories of the path travelled, and the vision of what is ahead of me. Without you, I can be vulnerable, but with you, I am invincible!

ACKNOWLEDGEMENTS

I've had the privilege of working for remarkable organizations. I am proud of the work we did together to lead with intent and have a positive impact on our employees, our business and our communities. The success we celebrated together gave me strength and confidence. The failures we shared became my biggest opportunities to learn, and the reason I wrote this business memoir. For each and every one of those opportunities, I am grateful. For the people who became part of this journey, I am blessed.

To my phenomenal publishing, editing and e-learning team: Melissa Wilson, Tom Johnson, Becky Blanton, Phil Elmore, Cheryl E. Booth, and Chelsea Byers. Thanks for helping me organize years of experiences in a way that others could receive it.

To the leaders, mentors, and coaches who continue to inspire me: Patricia Barlow, Eva Montalvo, Paul Richardson. I am honored to be the recipient of your wisdom and encouragement.

To the D&I colleagues and friends who reviewed some of the stories I shared in this book: thank you for ensuring my memories were as precise as the moments when we lived them together.

APPENDIX

This appendix contains a few more "how-to" tools and guidance on certain chapters of the book.

LEARNING & DEVELOPMENT TOOLS

THE 5 DUALITIES OF DIVERSITY & INCLUSION

	From INTENT		To IMPACT
1	Connect	&	Learn
2	Think	&	Know
3	Pain	&	Possibility
4	Risk	&	Invest
5	Perform	&	Innovate

PART 1: FINDING YOUR IDENTITY
IN DIVERSITY

THE FIRST TIME YOU FELT DIFFERENT

Everyone has personal experiences, encounters, and reflections that shape their lives. Some people are aware of those moments, while others are not. You can identify those past moments in your own life by starting with questions like these:

- What was a moment in my life when I felt different?
- What was a moment in my life when I felt less than others?
- What was a moment in my life when I felt more than others?

Then, move on to your "now" moments:

- When do I feel powerful?
  - What am I doing, or where am I when I feel that way?
  - Who do I feel most comfortable, confident, and powerful around?
- When do I feel "less than," diminished, demoralized, or uncertain?
  - What is happening in those moments?
  - Who am I around when this happens?
- Compare the two...
  - How would you feel if being powerful happened most of the time in your life?
  - How would you feel if being diminished happened most of the time in your life?

PART 2: THE 5 DUALITIES OF DIVERSITY & INCLUSION

DUALITY 1: CONNECT AND LEARN

NO THREAT, EARLY GAIN

Set a Goal

- For the next 21 days, set a goal for yourself to *learn intentionally* about a diversity dimension (e.g.: race, ethnicity, gender, national origin, disability, introverts, a disability, sexual orientation, generational differences, religion, social status / castes, adoption parenting) you would like to know more about. It should be something that is different from your own personal experience—ideally, a dimension that identifies people you know personally (members of your team, your family, your friends).
  - Identify and select three "no-threat" activities where you have no risk of public failure, such as watching a documentary or reading a book about the diversity dimension you chose as the objective of your learning, of your *discovery.*
  - Write down what you learn and how that new awareness may change your approach in your next exchange with someone who represents that same difference.

Create a Habit

- Set a second 21-day goal on another diversity dimension you would like to know more about.

- Identify a **trusted partner** (e.g.: friend, family member, colleague) and let them know about the 21-day goal you established for yourself. You may even want to share what you have learned.

LEARN FROM DEEP IMMERSION

Establish a common purpose / intent with your team:

- Necessary for your organization to thrive and grow
- Focus on development of potential, not improvement of performance

Make it simple, but supported:

- You don't need to have much structure. Conversations should flow easily.
- Make sure you have capable facilitators. Emotions and sensitivities can and will run high.
- Encourage (but don't force) the team to have a dialogue: share their experiences and ask about the experiences of others.

Make it Voluntary:

- Let curiosity grow, starting with those who already want to learn, but would otherwise be fearful to do so.

Lead by example:

- Senior leaders are participants / learners in the session. They are the first ones to share their vulnerabilities and what they want to learn, and ask others for their support.
- Nobody is expected to be "perfect" when addressing human differences, but they will all be expected to be curious about them.

It's ok to have fun!

- At its best, learning is an enjoyable experience.
- Diversity and inclusion don't always have to be about the most difficult experiences of human conflict.

UNLEARN TO LEARN

As an individual:

- When you seek to understand what makes someone different from you, be clear about your true **motivation.**
- Let that motivation guide your **curiosity**.
- Identify a partner, a buddy, who can help you feel **safe** in your exploration of cultural differences.

As a leader, ask your team:

- What is a true **motivation** you may have to learn and better understand human differences?
- What could I do to create a **safe work environment** where we can all be **curious**, to explore differences that could be divisive in our team?

DUALITY 2: THINK AND KNOW

KNOW AND WIN, ASSUME AND FAIL

Be aware of when you might be jumping to conclusions:

- When you use previous experiences to *think* that you *know* what may be happening under new circumstances. This is particularly important when you're **making judgments** about someone who you see as "different" from you.

Slow down to test your assumptions:

- If others are quick to agree with your point of view, this doesn't necessarily mean that you're right. Check yourself: This could be a sign that you're asking people who are **"very much like you."**

ATTRACT THEM AND RETAIN THEM

Seek and discuss turnover data of diverse talent:

- This will tell you if you have a back door that is draining your hiring efforts on diverse talent.

- Identify areas where you need to take action to reverse a negative trend of people leaving or being pushed away from the organization.

- Evaluate any signs of systemic bias that may be present in your human resources processes or management practices.

Challenge your thinking:

- Seek opportunities to immerse yourself in forums or experiences that can give you first-hand knowledge (verified observations), instead of over relying on limited or previous information.

DUALITY 3: PAIN AND POSSIBILITY

To have a more positive impact in addressing **social issues related to Diversity & Inclusion**, consider the following "do's" and "don'ts" as your initial guidance:

DO	DON'T
PREPARE	*ASSUME*
Anticipate: If you have not done so already, create company guidance with criteria on when and how your organization will address and respond to social issues. Your D&I partner, HR Business partner, Corporate Communications and Corporate Responsibility departments should collaborate in developing this guidance.	Don't think you can address each social issue individually, as it comes. Without proper and agreed-upon guidance on how to address them, you run the risk of being inconsistent in your approach. It is likely that you will have a variety of social issues that have impact on your D&I practices and company reputation.
Identify: Ask how a social issue / incident impacts your key stakeholders (e.g.: employees, customers, communities where you operate).	Don't assume that if you're not "hearing about it" before you ask, that a concern is not present. As a rule of thumb, don't think that "no 'noise' is good news."
Evaluate: How your company values, diversity and inclusion and corporate social responsibility strategies relate to the social issue under discussion.	Don't think your senior leaders and people managers will know what to do or say in these instances. You don't have to respond to every social issue, but should have discussed them and have a

	company's point of view that you can share with people managers.
Determine: If your response / action / expression on the social issue will be internal (only), external or both. Be mindful that, in the age of social media, your internal communications can (and most likely will) become visible outside your organization.	Don't assume that an internal response implies that you're "forced" to make an externally focused communication as well. You can decide on the extent of your response.

DO	DON'T
COMMUNICATE	*IMPROVISE*
Acknowledge: Let your team know that you understand there may be different opinions and reactions to the social issue under discussion (as appropriate), but focus on acknowledging the *impact* it has on a specific segment of the community. Use personal stories to authentically share how you're processing the specific issue, in a way that relates to the negative impact it has on other individuals as well as the community.	Don't improvise explanations about the *intent* of each party involved in a social issue. Don't judge the adequacy of the reaction(s) of those impacted by a social issue. In most instances, you will not have enough information on the topic, or truly relate to the life circumstances of those negatively impacted by a social issue.
Engage: As a leader and as an organization make time to listen to the concerns and questions from key stakeholders, either in	Don't think that a social issue should only be addressed with the those who are more visibly impacted by issues of social inequity (e.g.: Men also care about

individual conversations or team meetings. • Gather input from employees and other key stakeholders about resources that would best support them. • Communicate the availability of these internal resources.	incidents of domestic violence against women; White employees may also feel and acknowledge the emotional impact that racial profiling has on people of color; Violence against the LGBTQ community is also felt deeply by their allies).
Engage your employee resource groups (ERGs), industry / community colleagues and non-government organizations (NGOs), to get an internal and also an external perspective on the issue (as appropriate). Empower your ERGs to serve as a barometer that keeps you informed of social pressures that impact your workforce, so you can better plan for actions needed in times of social unrest.	Don't rely only on your own ideas to identify what type of resource would be most helpful to your employees and key stakeholders. People may ask for simple things you may have not even considered (e.g.: a collective minute of silence, your support of having further conversations about the issue at hand, a "support signature board" in the lobby of your building).
Respond: Your ability to respectfully listen to another person's story and perspective matters to them. Expressing your concern for the impact the social issue has on them does not imply you need to agree with their point of view.	Don't improvise your response to every story or every comment. When emotions run high, there can be polarizing points of view. This is not the time to "wing it." Plan your approach, to ensure your response is authentic, but also balanced.
TAKE ACTION	*STAY ON THE SIDELINES*
Support: Identify how you and your organization can have a	As difficult as it is to address social issues of inequality and

positive impact in the community, by supporting, partnering and/ or funding organizations that work to create greater equality in society.	discrimination, business leaders hold a privileged position in having positive impact. Staying on the sidelines of social issues is no longer an option, if you intend to successfully and effectively lead a team or lead a company.

DUALITY 4: RISK AND INVEST

KNOW YOUR RISK TOLERANCE

As a people manager, do a self-check…

1. Before your next **succession planning** or **promotion planning** process, take note on how you would describe the talent within your team:

    - Which ones would you describe as "people you consider a risk"? Why do you see them as a risk?

    - Which ones would you describe as "people you should invest in"? Why do you see them as worthy of your investment?

2. Do you see any disparities between people who are "more like you" and people who are "different from you?"

3. For those you identify as a "risk," what could you do to shift to an "investor mindset" with that person?

    - What actions can you take to manage those differences as *assets*, versus *deficits*?

DIVERSIFY YOUR TALENT PORTFOLIO

As a people manager, take a look at your team:

- Which differences are more prominent within your team?
- Which differences are missing?
    - **Internal:** gender, race, ethnicity, generational, thinking style, culture, language, etc.
    - **External:** geographical location, educational background, etc.
    - **Organizational:** tenure in the organization, career path followed, etc.

Be conscious of the "illusion" of diversity: the false impression of "being diverse" because "diversity numbers say so."

- Do you *truly* have a diverse team? A diversified talent portfolio? or
- Is your team a group of "sameness" of a different color, gender, ethnicity, educational background, etc.?

DUALITY 5: PERFORM AND INNOVATE

INCLUSIVE LEADERS REQUIRED

Innovation happens when different ideas are put together to create something new or something better. Consider the following D&I behaviors that can spark and ignite innovation within your team:

| BEHAVIORS THAT DRIVE INNOVATION ||
DIVERSITY	*INCLUSION*
1. Challenge traditional thinking of what is considered "best talent."	1. Strive to be an "idea builder," not an "idea killer." Ask *"how could we make that happen?"*, instead of saying *"that will not work."*
2. Identify differences amongst your team members that can bring creative perspectives to your work.	2. In meetings, seek everyone's point of view, at their own time, in their own way (verbally, in writing, with visual aids, etc.).
3. Expedite the development of talent who can bring different perspectives to your team.	3. When engaging with colleagues from different cultures, avoid colloquial references or analogies that may not resonate with them.
4. Engage employees at lower levels of the organization in management meetings, to seek their input on challenges you're working on.	4. Ask your team what "traditional ideas" or cultural norms are getting in the way of "new ideas" within your team, within your company.
5. Engage diverse suppliers who can add different perspectives to your business, even more if you have headcount constraints to diversify your team.	5. Share and recognize the value of people who explore/execute on new ideas, even if they are not immediately successful.

PART 3: EVOLUTION AND REVOLUTION

THE CHOICE IS YOURS

Evolution Is Gradual	Revolution Is Radical
In leading a *D&I evolution,* your role is to: **enable, support and track progress.**	In leading *a D&I revolution,* your role is to: **provide a vision, energize, drive a sense of urgency.**
For example: Support and require progress reports on development and advancement of diverse talent.	*For example: Hold yourself and others accountable and visibly recognize significant progress on diversity and inclusion metrics. Require that each member of your team does as well.*
What *D&I evolution* will you lead?	What *D&I revolution* will you lead?

- What personal, leadership or social impact do you want to have?
- When are you starting?
- What is your first step?

NOTES

[1] Deepak Chopra, *The Book of Secrets: Unlocking the Hidden Dimensions of Your Life* (New York: Three Rivers Press, 2004).

[2] Paul Taylor, Mark Hugo Lopez, Jessica Martínez, and Gabriel Velasco, "Identity, Pan-Ethnicity, and Race," Pew Research Center, April 4, 2012, https://www.pewresearch.org/hispanic/2012/04/04/ii-identity-pan-ethnicity-and-race/.

[3] Kenji Yoshino, "Covering," *Yale Law Journal* 111, no. 4 (January 2002): 771–939, https://www.yalelawjournal.org/article/covering.

[4] Kelly-Ann Allen and Peggy Kern, "The Importance of Belonging Across Life: A Developmental Perspective of Our Need to Belong," *Psychology Today,* June 20, 2019, https://www.psychologytoday.com/us/blog/sense-belonging/201906/the-importance-belonging-across-life.

[5] Elizabeth Prine Pauls, "Assimilation," *Encyclopedia Britannica,* accessed July 25, 2020, https://www.britannica.com/topic/assimilation-society.

[6] Nicki Lisa Cole, "Understanding Acculturation and Why It Happens," *Thought Co.,* November 8, 2019, https://www.thoughtco.com/acculturation-definition-3026039.

[7] Kendra Cherry, "What Is a Single-Blind Study?" *Explore Psychology,* July 26, 2017, https://www.explorepsychology.com/single-blind-study.

[8] Kevin Daum, "22 Inspiring Quotes from United States Supreme Court Justices." *Inc.,* March 20, 2017, https://www.inc.com/kevin-daum/22-inspiring-quotes-from-united-states-supreme-court-justices.html.

[9] Justin Bariso, "How Emotional Intelligence Fueled Everette Taylor's Rise to the Top," *Inc.,* September 26, 2016, https://www.inc.com/justin-bariso/how-emotional-intelligence-helped-everette-taylor-become-a-millennial-marketing-.html.

[10] Kevin Payne, "Rags to Riches: 4 Amazing Black Startup Founders Who Will Inspire You," *Blavity,* April 13, 2018, https://blavity.com/rags-to-riches-4-amazing-black-startup-founders-that-will-inspire-you?category1=community-submitted&subCat=business-entrepreneurship.

[11] "Colonel Harland Sanders," *Biography,* updated April 24, 2020, https://www.biography.com/business-figure/colonel-harland-sanders.

[12] Kerri Lee Alexander, "Patsy Mink," National Women's History Museum, accessed July 25, 2020, www.womenshistory.org/education-resources/biographies/patsy-mink.

[13] Payne, "Rags to Riches."

[14] Holly Slade, "How This Man Built a $3M Business a Year After Four Years in Prison," *Forbes,* August 21, 2014, https://www.forbes.com/sites/hollieslade/2014/08/21/how-this-man-built-a-3m-business-a-year-on-from-four-years-in-prison/#e0421c16780b.

15 Bianca Taylor, "Flamin' Hot Cheetos: The Humble Beginnings of a Junk Food," KQED, March 15, 2019, https://www.kqed.org/news/11732648/flamin-hot-cheetos-the-humble-beginnings-of-a-junk-food21.

16 "Powering Change: Women in Innovation and Creativity: Olga Gonzalez-Sanabria," CPA Global, accessed July 25, 2020, https://www.cpaglobal.com/women-innovators/olga-d-gonzalez-sanabria.

17 Sarah Ashlock, "Ann Tsukamoto: The Truth About Stem Cells," *On The Dot Woman,* May 3, 2019, https://onthedotwoman.com/woman/ann-tsukamoto.

18 Amanda Schaffer. "The Remarkable Career of Shirley Ann Jackson," *MIT Technology Review,* December 19, 2017, https://www.technologyreview.com/s/609692/the-remarkable-career-of-shirley-ann-jackson/.

19 Bianca Taylor, "Flamin' Hot Cheetos: The Humble Beginnings of a Junk Food," KQED, March 15, 2019, https://www.kqed.org/news/11732648/flamin-hot-cheetos-the-humble-beginnings-of-a-junk-food21.

20 Adam Grant, *Originals: How Non-Conformists Move the World* (New York: Penguin Books, 2017).

21 Frans Johansson, *The Medici Effect: What Elephants and Epidemics Can Teach Us About Innovation* (Cambridge, MA: Harvard Business School, 2006), 18–20.

22 Anesa "Nes" Diaz-Uda, Carmen Medina, and Beth Schill, "Diversity's New Frontier: Diversity of Thought and the Future of the Workforce," Deloitte, accessed July 25, 2020, https://www2.deloitte.com/us/en/insights/topics/talent/diversitys-new-frontier.html#.

23 "Difference Between Behavioral Psychology and Cognitive Psychology," *Psychology School Guide,* accessed July 25, 2020, https://www.psychologyschool-guide.net/guides/difference-between-behavioral-psychology-and-cognitive-psychology.

24 "MBTI Basics," Myers and Briggs Foundation, accessed July 25, 2020, https://www.myersbriggs.org/my-mbti-personality-type/mbti-basics.

25 "DiSC Overview," DiSC Profile, accessed July 25, 2020, https://www.discprofile.com/what-is-disc/overview.

26 "Insights Discovery," Insights, accessed July 25, 2020, https://www.insights.com/us/products/insights-discovery/.

27 "Clifton Strengths," Gallup, accessed July 25, 2020, https://www.gallup.com/cliftonstrengths/en/strengthsfinder.aspx.

28 Grant, *Originals.*

29 Psychology School Guide.

30 From a global perspective, *black* refers to individuals of that race in different countries, who therefore don't self-identify as *African American.*

31 Josh Bersin, "Why Diversity and Inclusion Will Be a Top Priority for 2016," *Forbes,* December 6, 2015, https://www.forbes.com/sites/joshbersin/2015/12/06/why-diversity-and-inclusion-will-be-a-top-priority-for-2016/#11fb5e7a2ed5.

32 "Waiter, Is That Inclusion in My Soup? A New Recipe to Improve Business Performance," Deloitte, May 2013, https://www2.deloitte.com/content/dam/Deloitte/au/Documents/human-capital/deloitte-au-hc-diversity-inclusion-soup-0513.pdf.

33 Vivian Hunt, Dennis Layton, and Sara Prince, "Why Diversity Matters," McKinsey and Company, January 1, 2015, https://www.mckinsey.com/business-functions/organization/our-insights/why-diversity-matters.

34 "A Starting Point: Diversity and Inclusion at Limeade," Limeade, accessed July 25, 2020, https://www.limeade.com/en/2017/11/starting-point-diversity-inclusion-limeade.

35 Dorie Clark and Christie Smith, "Help Your Employees Be Themselves at Work," *Harvard Business Review,* November 3, 2014, https://hbr.org/2014/11/help-your-employees-be-themselves-at-work.

36 Julie Sweet and Ellyn Shook, "Getting to Equal 2020: The Hidden Value of Culture Makers," Accenture, accessed July 25, 2020, https://www.accenture.com/us-en/about/inclusion-diversity/_acnmedia/Thought-Leadership-Assets/PDF-2/Accenture-Getting-To-Equal-2020-Research-Report.pdf.

37 Jerry Sternin and Robert Choo, "The Power of Positive Deviancy," *Harvard Business Review,* January–February 2020, https://hbr.org/2000/01/the-power-of-positive-deviancy.

38 "Habit 5: Seek First to Understand, Then to Be Understood," Franklin Covey, accessed July 25, 2020. https://www.franklincovey.com/the-7-habits/habit-5.html.

39 "Reflective Listening," *People Communicating,* accessed July 25, 2020, http://www.people-communicating.com/reflective-listening.html.

40 Jessica Gross, "Reasoning Is Sharper in a Foreign Language," *Scientific American*, November 1, 2012, https://www.scientificamerican.com/article/reasoning-is-sharper-in-a-foreign-language.

41 Michael Erard, "The Reason You Discriminate against Foreign Accents Starts with What They Do to Your Brain," *Quartz,* February 25, 2016, https://qz.com/624335/the-reason-you-discriminate-against-foreign-accents-starts-with-what-they-do-to-your-brain.

42 Lisa Bonos, "Why Do Americans Think British Accents Are Sexy?" *Washington Post,* May 17, 2018, https://www.washingtonpost.com/news/soloish/wp/2018/05/17/why-do-americans-think-the-british-accent-is-sexy.

43 Kristen Adaway, "Americans Can't Get Enough of Southern Accents, Despite the Stereotypes," *Huffington Post,* August 7, 2018, https://www.huffpost.com/entry/americans-love-southern-accents_n_5b5f6cffe4b0de86f499dd11.

[44] Antonio Benítez-Burraco, "How the Language We Speak Affects the Way We Think," *Psychology Today,* February 2, 2017, https://www.psychologyto-day.com/us/blog/the-biolinguistic-turn/201702/how-the-language-we-speak-affects-the-way-we-think.

[45] Devyani Sharma, Erez Levon, Dominic Watt, Yang Ye, and Amanda Cardoso, "Methods for the Study of Accent Bias and Access to Elite Professions," *Journal of Language and Discrimination* 3, no. 2 (2019), https://journals.equinoxpub.com/JLD/article/viewFile/39979/pdf.

[46] Raquel Magelhães, "Accent Discrimination: Let's Call the Whole Thing Off," *Understanding with Unbabel,* June 25, 2019, https://unbabel.com/blog/language-foreign-accents-discrimination.

[47] Anese Cavanaugh, *Contagious Culture* (New York: McGraw Hill Education, 2015).

[48] "The Four Stages of Competence," *Training Industry,* May 11, 2017, https://trainingindustry.com/wiki/strategy-alignment-and-planning/the-four-stages-of-competence.

[49] Forbes Coaches Council, "11 Assessments Every Executive Should Take," *Forbes,* May 1, 2018, https://www.forbes.com/sites/forbescoachescouncil/2018/05/01/11-assessments-every-executive-should-take/#2a7d19a17a51.

[50] "Michelangelo Buonarroti," EDinformatics, accessed July 25, 2020, https://www.edinformatics.com/great_thinkers/michelangelo.htm.

[51] Mike Noon, "Pointless Diversity Training: Unconscious Bias, New Racism and Agency," *Work, Employment and Society* 32, no. 1 (February 2018): 198–209, https://doi.org/10.1177/0950017017719841.

[52] Anjana Sreedhar, "The Inspiring Story of How Venus Williams Helped Win Equal Pay for Women Players at Wimbledon," *Women in the World,* July 10, 2015.

[53] Michelle Garcia, "Five Years Later, Michael Sam is Doing Just Fine, Thanks," *Out,* March 25, 2019, https://www.out.com/sports/2019/3/22/michael-sam-now-football.

[54] Victor Mather, "Colin Kaepernick Is Unemployed. Is It Because of His Arm, or His Knee?" *New York Times,* March 27, 2017, https://www.nytimes.com/2017/03/27/sports/football/free-agent-colin-kaepernick-national-anthem-protest.html.

[55] Sean Gregory, "Athlete of the Year: U.S. Women's Soccer Team," *Time,* December 11, 2019, https://time.com/athlete-of-the-year-2019-us-womens-soccer-team.

[56] "Intergroup Dialogue Project," Cornell University, accessed July 25, 2020, https://idp.cornell.edu.

[57] "Intergroup Dialogue," Syracuse University, accessed July 25, 2020, https://intergroupdialogue.syr.edu.

[58] K. Anders Ericsson, Robert R. Hoffman, Aaron Kozbelt, and A. Mark Williams, eds., *The Cambridge Handbook of Expertise and Expert Performance* (Cambridge, UK: Cambridge University Press, 2018).

59 Malcolm Gladwell, *Outliers: The Story of Success* (New York: Little, Brown and Company, 2008).

60 Frans Johannsson, *The Click Moment: Seizing Opportunity in an Unpredictable World* (New York: Portfolio, 2012).

61 Daniel Goleman, Richard Boyatzis, and Annie McKee, *Primal Leadership: Unleashing the Power of Emotional Intelligence* (Boston: Harvard Business Review Press, 2013).

62 Michael Hvisdos, "Leadership and the Curiosity Quotient," *Management Issues*, April 16, 2015, https://www.management-issues.com/opinion/7048/leadership-and-the-curiosity-quotient.

63 Kenneth Mikkelsen and Harold Jarche, "The Best Leaders Are Constant Learners," *Harvard Business Review*, October 16, 2015, https://hbr.org/2015/10/the-best-leaders-are-constant-learners.

64 Andy Molinsky and Sujin Jang, "To Connect Across Cultures, Find Out What You Have in Common," *Harvard Business Review*, January 20, 2016, https://hbr.org/2016/01/to-connect-across-cultures-find-out-what-you-have-in-common.

65 Christopher G. Coutlee, Anastasia Kiyonaga, Franziska M. Korb, Scott A. Huettel, and Tobias Egner, "Reduced Risk-Taking Following Disruption of the Intraparietal Sulcus," *Frontiers in Neuroscience*, December 23, 2016, https://doi.org/10.3389/fnins.2016.00588.

66 "The Power of Employee Resource Groups in the Workplace," Workforce Opportunity Services, October 31, 2018, https://www.wforce.org/news/the-power-of-ergs-employee-resource-groups-in-the-workplace?gclid=CjwKCAjwhOD0BRAQEi-wAK7JHmIP_RTYO0bJr7DpVjVXepcjpBFr__veww_aRnwSAc02EW00luHPd-DRoCm_QQAvD_BwE.

67 Avivah Wittenberg-Cox, "Deloitte's Radical Attempt to Reframe Diversity," *Harvard Business Review*, August 3, 2017, https://hbr.org/2017/08/deloittes-radical-attempt-to-reframe-diversity.

68 Molinsky and Jang, "To Connect Across Cultures."

69 Jason S. Moser, "How Your Brain Reacts to Mistakes Depends on Your Mindset," Association for Psychological Science, September 29, 2011, https://www.psychologicalscience.org/news/releases/how-the-brain-reacts-to-mistakes.html.

70 "The Deep South," Cambridge Dictionary, accessed July 25, 2020, https://dictionary.cambridge.org/us/dictionary/english/deep-south.

71 Kara, "The History and Meaning of African Head Wraps," Natural Curlies, October 7, 2018, https://www.naturalcurlies.com/the-history-and-meaning-of-african-head-wraps.

72 "What Is Bonded Labour?" Anti-Slavery, accessed July 25, 2020, https://www.anti-slavery.org/slavery-today/bonded-labour.

73 "Sawubona: An African Tribe's Beautiful Greeting," Exploring Your Mind, October 18, 2018, https://exploringyourmind.com/sawubona-african-tribe-greeting.

74 "Ubuntu, Explained by Nelson Mandela," interview with Tim Modise, May 24, 2006, https://commons.wikimedia.org/wiki/File:Experience_ubuntu.ogv.

75 "Human Uniqueness and the African Spirit of Ubuntu, Desmond Tutu," Templeton Prize, April 3, 2013, https://youtu.be/0wZtfqZ271w.

76 "An Overview of the African-American Experience," Constitutional Rights Foundation, accessed July 25, 2020, https://www.crf-usa.org/black-history-month/an-overview-of-the-african-american-experience.

77 Linda Jones, "More About the Kitchen," Naturally Curly, July 1, 2008, https://www.naturallycurly.com/curlreading/kinky-hair-type-4a/naturally-speaking-more-about-the-kitchen.

78 Princess Jones, "8 Things You Always Wanted to Know About Black Women's Hair," The Mash-Up Americans, accessed July 25, 2020, http://www.mashupamericans.com/issues/8-things-always-wanted-know-black-womens-hair.

79 Linda D. Sharkey, Nazneen Razi, Robert A. Cooke, and Peter Barge, *Winning with Transglobal Leadership* (New York: McGraw-Hill Education, 2012).

80 Arash Javanbakht and Linda Saab, "What Happens in the Brain When We Feel Fear," *Smithsonian Magazine,* October 27, 2017, https://www.smithsonianmag.com/science-nature/what-happens-brain-feel-fear-180966992.

81 Ian Leslie, *Curious: The Desire to Know and Why Your Future Depends on It* (New York: Basic Books, 2014).

82 Pierre-Yves Oudeyer, "The Mysteries of Human Curiosity-Driven Learning and the Challenges of Translational Educational Sciences," *CDS Newsletter* 15, no. 1 (spring 2018): 1. http://celestekidd.com/papers/CDSNL-V15-N1.pdf.

83 Saga Briggs, "Why Curiosity Is Essential to Motivation," InformEd, November 17, 2017, https://www.opencolleges.edu.au/informed/features/curiosity-essential-motivation.

84 Andy Molinsky and Ernest Gundling, "How to Build Trust on Your Cross-Cultural Team," *Harvard Business Review,* June 28, 2016, https://hbr.org/2016/06/how-to-build-trust-on-your-cross-cultural-team.

85 David Cooperrider, "What Is Appreciative Inquiry?" David Cooperrider and Associates, accessed July 25, 2020, https://www.davidcooperrider.com/ai-process/.

86 Jenny Clark, "Seven Steps to Become a Global Citizen," GVI, accessed July 25, 2020, https://www.gviusa.com/blog/7-steps-to-become-a-global-citizen.

87 *Chasing Coral,* directed by Jeff Orlowski, written by Vickie Curtis (Netflix, 2017), https://chasingcoral.com.

88 Brynn Holland, "How Activists Plotted the First Gay Pride Parades," *History,* updated June 28, 2019, https://www.history.com/news/how-activists-plotted-the-first-gay-pride-parades.

89 Deb Peterson, "Overview and Definition of Experiential Learning," *Thought Co.,* updated May 9, 2019. https://www.thoughtco.com/what-is-experiential-learning-31324.

[90] "Stonewall National Monument, New York," National Park Service, updated June 5, 2020, https://www.nps.gov/ston/index.htm.

[91] Daniel Kahneman, *Thinking, Fast and Slow* (New York: Farrar, Straus, and Giroux, 2013).

[92] "The Ladder of Inference: How to Avoid Jumping to Conclusions," Mind Tools, accessed July 25, 2020, https://www.mindtools.com/pages/article/newTMC_91.htm.

[93] Shane McFeely and Ben Wigert, "This Fixable Problem Costs U.S. Businesses $1 Trillion," Gallup, March 13, 2019, https://www.gallup.com/workplace/247391/fixable-problem-costs-businesses-trillion.aspx.

[94] "Can Glassdoor Reviews Impact Your Company and Your Recruiting Efforts?" Strategic HR Inc., September 18, 2018, https://strategichrinc.com/can-glassdoor-reviews-impact-your-company-and-your-recruiting-efforts.

[95] Kent Campbell, "Corporate Reputation: What, How, and Why," Business 2 Community, July 16, 2018, https://www.business2community.com/public-relations/corporate-reputation-what-how-and-why-02091720.

[96] "Shocking Employee Turnover Statistics," Reflektive, August 27, 2018, https://www.reflektive.com/blog/shocking-turnover-statistics/.

[97] "USS Ronald Reagan (CVN 76)," United States Navy, accessed July 25, 2020, https://www.navy.mil/local/cvn76/.

[98] Brian Harmsen and Michelle Winkley, "Break the Language Barrier Between Recruiters and Veterans," ERE Media, October 8, 2019, https://www.ere.net/break-the-language-barrier-between-recruiters-and-veterans/.

[99] Justin Constantine, "Guide to Veteran Hiring: 8 Facts to Break Down Barriers and Stereotypes," SHRM, August 8, 2018, www.shrm.org/ResourcesAndTools/hr-topics/talent-acquisition/Pages/Guide-to-Veteran-Hiring-8-Facts-to-Break-Down-Barriers-and-Stereotypes.aspx.

[100] "7 Common Misconceptions About Veterans (and Why They're Harmful)," Leader Quest, May 15, 2020, https://www.leaderquestonline.com/blog/misconceptions-about-veterans/.

[101] Michelle S. Moses and Laura Dudley Jenkins, "Affirmative Action Around the World," *The Conversation,* August 7, 2017, https://theconversation.com/affirmative-action-around-the-world-82190.

[102] Maggie Gnadt, "Why a Great Company Reputation Is Important," Reputation Management, November 25, 2017, https://www.reputationmanagement.com/blog/negative-company-reputation-affects-business/.

[103] Greg Depersio, "The Best (and Worst) Companies for Workplace Diversity," *Investopedia,* updated April 21, 2020, https://www.investopedia.com/articles/professionals/072815/best-and-worst-companies-workplace-diversity.asp.

[104] "Magnet for Talent: Managing Diversity as a Reputational Risk and Business Opportunity," PwC UK, accessed July 25, 2020, https://www.pwc.co.uk/human-resource-services/assets/documents/diversity-and-inclusion-reputation-2017.pdf.

[105] "The Cost of Silence: Why More CEOs Are Speaking Out in the Trump Era," *New Zealand Herald,* February 18, 2017, https://www.nzherald.co.nz/business/news/article.cfm?c_id=3&objectid=11803318.

[106] Ariel Zambelich and Alyson Hurt, "3 Hours in Orlando: Piecing Together an Attack and Its Aftermath," *The Two-Way,* NPR, June 26, 2016, https://www.npr.org/2016/06/16/482322488/orlando-shooting-what-happened-update.

[107] "There Are 44 NFL Players Who Have Been Accused of Sexual or Physical Assault," *Vice,* December 8, 2015, https://www.vice.com/en_us/article/8qwpm4/2015-nfl-report.

[108] Caitlin Dickerson, "What Is DACA? And How Did It End Up in the Supreme Court?" *New York Times,* July 3, 2020, https://www.nytimes.com/2019/11/12/us/daca-supreme-court.html.

[109] P. R. Lockhart, "Living While Black and the Criminalization of Blackness," *Vox,* August 1, 2018, https://www.vox.com/explainers/2018/8/1/17616528/racial-profiling-police-911-living-while-black.

[110] Elizabeth Segran, "Escalating Sweatshop Protests Keep Nike Sweating," *Fast Company,* July 28, 2017, https://www.fastcompany.com/40444836/escalating-sweatshop-protests-keep-nike-sweating.

[111] Leighanna Shirey, "Major Oil Companies Accused of Illegally Dumping Toxic Waste," Citizen Truth, January 19, 2019, https://citizentruth.org/major-oil-companies-accused-of-illegally-dumping-toxic-waste/.

[112] Valeria Pelet, "Puerto Rico's Invisible Health Crisis," *The Atlantic,* September 3, 2016, https://www.theatlantic.com/politics/archive/2016/09/vieques-invisible-health-crisis/498428/.

[113] Josh Bersin, "Yes, CEOs, You Do Need to Speak Up on Social Issues," *Forbes,* September 5, 2018, https://www.forbes.com/sites/joshbersin/2018/09/05/yes-ceos-you-do-need-to-speak-up-on-social-issues/#4b0c5b8c5898.

[114] Adriana Galant and Simon Cadez, "Corporate Social Responsibility and Financial Performance Relationship: A Review of Measurement Approaches," *Economic Research-Ekonomska Istraživanja* 30, no. 1 (January 2017): 676–93, https://doi.org/10.1080/1331677X.2017.1313122.

[115] David P. Baron, Maretno Harjoto, and Hoje Jo, "The Economics and Politics of Corporate Social Performance" (working paper no. 1993, Stanford Business, 2009), https://www.gsb.stanford.edu/faculty-research/working-papers/economics-politics-corporate-social-performance.

[116] Sukanya Chetty, Rebekah Raidoo, and Yudhvir Seetharam, "The Impact of Corporate Social Responsibility on Firms' Financial Performance in South Africa," *Contemporary Economics* 9, no. 2 (2015): 193–214, https://doi.org/10.5709/ce.1897-9254.167.

[117] Valerie Bolden-Barrett, "Study: 81% of Millennials Want Companies to Be Good Corporate Citizens," HR Dive, March 2, 2017, https://www.hrdive.com/news/study-81-of-millennials-want-companies-to-be-good-corporate-citizens/437220/.

[118] Sunny Bonnell, "Mad at Colin Kaepernick? That's Exactly Why He Should Be Your Leadership Role Model," *Inc.,* September 5, 2018, https://www.inc.com/sunny-bonnell/why-colin-kaepernicks-nike-ad-sets-new-bar-for-leaders.html?cid=readmore-text_ab.

[119] Anthony López, *The Legacy Leader as Superhero: Legacy Woman* (Bloomington, IN: Author House, 2018).

[120] Dina Gerdeman, "Religion in the Workplace: What Managers Need to Know," *Forbes,* October 4, 2018, https://www.forbes.com/sites/hbsworking-knowledge/2018/10/04/religion-in-the-workplace-what-managers-need-to-know/#7c2f0df2597b.

[121] Dionne Searcey, "At George Floyd Memorial, an Anguished Call for Change," *New York Times,* updated June 9, 2020, https://www.nytimes.com/2020/06/04/us/floyd-memorial-funeral.html.

[122] "Ava DuVernay Reveals Why She Was So Shocked by Seeing George Floyd's Murder," *Just Jared,* June 8, 2020, http://www.justjared.com/2020/06/08/ava-duvernay-reveals-why-she-was-so-shocked-by-seeing-george-floyds-murder.

[123] Blake Freas, "Mayors: COVID-19 Followed by Second 'Pandemic' of Police Relations," *Cronkite News,* June 11, 2020, https://cronkitenews.az-pbs.org/2020/06/11/mayors-covid-19-followed-by-second-pandemic-of-police-relations.

[124] Agata Sobkow, Jakub Traczyk, and Tomasz Zaleskiewicz, "The Affective Bases of Risk Perception: Negative Feelings and Stress Mediate the Relationship Between Mental Imagery and Risk Perception," *Frontiers in Psychology,* June 24, 2016, https://doi.org/10.3389/fpsyg.2016.00932.

[125] Patrick B. Healey, "The Psychology of the Stock Market and Investment Decisions," Kiplinger, January 28, 2019, https://www.kiplinger.com/article/invest-ing/t031-c032-s014-psychology-of-stock-market-and-investment-decision.html.

[126] Orman, Suze. "Financial Solutions for You." Suzeorman.com. Accessed July 5, 2020. https://www.suzeorman.com/

[127] Alexandra Twin, "Risk Tolerance," *Investopedia,* updated May 31, 2020, https://www.investopedia.com/terms/r/risktolerance.asp.

[128] Joan C. Williams and Marina Multhaup, "For Women and Minorities to Get Ahead, Managers Must Assign Work Fairly," *Harvard Business Review,* March 5, 2018, https://hbr.org/2018/03/for-women-and-minorities-to-get-ahead-managers-must-assign-work-fairly.

[129] Nick Lioudis, "The Importance of Diversification," *Investopedia,* updated August 15, 2019, https://www.investopedia.com/investing/importance-diversification/.

[130] Barb Darrow, "At the Ripe Age of 105, IBM Seeks to Reinvent Itself—Again," *Fortune,* June 16, 2016, https://fortune.com/longform/ibm-105-anniversary/.

[131] Oliver Kmia, "Why Kodak Died and Fujifilm Thrived: A Tale of Two Film Companies," PetaPixel, October 19, 2018, https://petapixel.com/2018/10/19/why-kodak-died-and-fujifilm-thrived-a-tale-of-two-film-companies/.

[132] Julie de la Kethulle de Ryhove, "What Is the 3 Horizons Model and How Can You Use It?" *Board of Innovation,* accessed July 25, 2020. https://www.boardofinnovation.com/blog/what-is-the-3-horizons-model-how-can-you-use-it.

[133] "Qualities of High-Performance Teams: Katzenbach and Smith," Team Building Portal, August 4, 2018, https://www.teambuildingportal.com/articles/effective-teams/qualities-high-performance-teams.

[134] Robert Iger, *The Ride of a Lifetime: Lessons Learned from 15 Years as CEO of the Walt Disney Company* (New York: Random House, 2019), 189.

[135] "Divergent Thinking: What It Is and How to Develop It," *Exploring Your Mind,* March 18, 2018, https://exploringyourmind.com/divergent-thinking-what-it-is.

[136] Lauren Landry, "How to Build an Effective Innovation Team," Northeastern University blog, October 25, 2017, https://www.northeastern.edu/graduate/blog/how-to-build-innovation-team.

[137] Nicki Lisa Cole, "Definition of Intersectionality: On the Intersecting Nature of Privileges and Oppression," *Thought Co.,* October 13, 2019, https://www.thoughtco.com/intersectionality-definition-3026353.

[138] Iger, *The Ride of a Lifetime.*

[139] Sharkey, et al., *Winning with Transglobal Leadership.*

[140] "Declaration of Independence," National Archives, accessed July 25, 2020, https://www.archives.gov/founding-docs/declaration-transcript.

[141] "Little People/Dwarfism," Respectability, accessed July 25, 2020, https://www.respectability.org/inclusion-toolkits/little-people-dwarfism/.

[142] "How Are the Terms Deaf, Deafened, Hard of Hearing, and Hearing Impaired Typically Used?" Disabilities, Opportunities, Internetworking, and Technology, University of Washington, updated April 30, 2019, https://www.washington.edu/doit/how-are-terms-deaf-deafened-hard-hearing-and-hearing-impaired-typically-used.

[143] "How Are the Terms Low Vision, Visually Impaired, and Blind Defined?" Disabilities, Opportunities, Internetworking, and Technology, University of Washington, updated April 30, 2019, https://www.washington.edu/doit/how-are-terms-low-vision-visually-impaired-and-blind-defined.

[144] "What Are Invisible Disabilities?" Disabled World, updated November 8, 2019, https://www.disabled-world.com/disability/types/invisible/.

[145] Paul Tesluk, "Leading Social Impact," *On Leadership: Insights from the University at Buffalo School of Management,* March 16, 2017, https://ubwp.buffalo.edu/school-of-management-leadership/2017/03/16/leading-social-impact/.